Certified Cybersecurity Technician (CCT) - Exam Prep

500 Questions and Explanations

Introduction

Welcome to "Certified Cybersecurity Technician (CCT) - Exam Prep: 500 Questions and Explanations," your essential guide to mastering the concepts and skills tested on the EC-Council's CCT exam. This book is meticulously designed to provide you with an in-depth review and practice that mimic the real exam environment, making it an invaluable resource for anyone preparing to certify their cybersecurity expertise.

Why This Book is a Must-Have:

- **Comprehensive Coverage:** With 500 carefully crafted questions and detailed explanations, this book covers every topic you'll encounter on the exam. Each question is designed to test your knowledge and ensure you understand both the concept and its application in real-world scenarios.

- **Practice Makes Perfect:** The variety of question formats—including multiple-choice, fill-in-the-gap, and scenario-based questions—provides a thorough practice experience that builds your confidence and readiness for the exam.

- **Expert Explanations:** The explanations accompanying each question don't just tell you the right answer—they explain why it's correct and why other options are not, deepening your understanding and analytical skills.

Achieving the CCT certification demonstrates your commitment to cybersecurity and your expertise in tackling current and emerging threats, making you a valuable asset to any organization and potentially leading to career growth and increased salary potential.

Practice Test

1. What is the correct command sequence to implement a security control that adheres to NIST SP 800-53 in a Linux system's firewall configuration to restrict unauthorized access?

A: iptables -A FORWARD -p tcp --dport 22 -j ACCEPT; iptables -P FORWARD DROP

B: sudo iptables -A INPUT -p tcp --dport 22 -j ACCEPT; sudo iptables -A INPUT -p tcp -j DROP

C: sudo firewall-cmd --zone=public --add-port=22/tcp --permanent; sudo firewall-cmd --reload

D: sudo ufw allow 22/tcp; sudo ufw deny all

Correct Answer: B

Explanation: The correct commands 'sudo iptables -A INPUT -p tcp --dport 22 -j ACCEPT' followed by 'sudo iptables -A INPUT -p tcp -j DROP' correctly configure the Linux firewall to allow SSH connections only and block all other incoming TCP connections, which adheres to the least privilege principle recommended by NIST SP 800-53 for restricting unauthorized access.

----

2. According to the ISO/IEC 27005 framework, which of these methods is most appropriate for assessing the impact and likelihood of potential threats during a risk assessment?

A: Qualitative risk assessment

B: Automated tools for risk analysis

C: Scenario-based risk assessment

D: Quantitative risk assessment

Correct Answer: A

Explanation: Qualitative risk assessment is highlighted in ISO/IEC 27005 as an appropriate method for assessing threats as it helps in evaluating the impact and likelihood based on subjective analysis of available data, which is crucial for setting priorities in risk management processes.

----

3. Fill in the blank: When configuring risk management protocols according to the guidelines in FIPS 199, it is crucial to classify information systems based on _____ to ensure proper security controls are applied.

A: type of data processed

B: user access levels and permissions

C: confidentiality, integrity, and availability levels

D: total system asset values

Correct Answer: C

Explanation: Classifying information systems based on 'confidentiality, integrity, and availability levels' is essential as per FIPS 199 to ensure that security controls are applied effectively according to the value and sensitivity of the information processed by the systems.

----

4. In a given scenario where an organization needs to comply with the GDPR risk management requirements, which of the following approaches should be prioritized when mapping data flow and identifying associated risks?

A: Conducting regular data protection impact assessments solely on high-risk processes

B: Implementing strong encryption for data at rest and in transit only

C: Updating privacy policies and user consent forms periodically

D: Creating a detailed data processing inventory including categories of personal data processed

Correct Answer: D

Explanation: Creating a detailed data processing inventory is essential for GDPR compliance as it helps organizations understand and map how personal data is handled, which is crucial for identifying risks to personal data and implementing appropriate security measures to mitigate them.

----

5. An organization is planning to enhance its risk response strategies. Which of the following best practices aligns with the COBIT framework for managing and optimizing IT risk?

A: Integrating risk management results with broader enterprise governance activities

B: Establishing a separate IT risk management department within the organization

C: Allocating a fixed annual budget to cover all IT-related risks

D: Reviewing IT risks on a predefined schedule, regardless of new projects or changes

Correct Answer: A

Explanation: Integrating risk management results with broader enterprise governance activities is a best practice under the COBIT framework as it ensures that IT risks are managed in alignment with enterprise goals and objectives, enhancing overall risk response strategies.

----

6. How would you configure a network scanning command to identify vulnerabilities within the corporate network?

A: arp-scan --interface=eth0 --localnet

B: netstat -tulpan | grep LISTEN

C: sudo traceroute -m 30 -q 1 192.168.1.1

D: nmap -sS -oX scan-results.xml 192.168.1.0/24

Correct Answer: D

Explanation: Using nmap -sS -oX scan-results.xml 192.168.1.0/24 configures Nmap to perform a stealth scan and output the results in XML format, which effectively identifies vulnerabilities by scanning all devices within the specified subnet without alerting the network's intrusion detection systems.

----

7. What is the most effective method to identify unauthorized access attempts in real-time on a Linux server?

A: Configuring syslog to monitor and alert on failed SSH login attempts

B: Setting up a cron job to regularly check /var/log/auth.log for new entries

C: Applying fail2ban to block IPs after multiple failed login attempts

D: Enabling two-factor authentication for all server access points

Correct Answer: A

Explanation: Configuring syslog to specifically monitor and send alerts for failed SSH login attempts provides real-time monitoring of unauthorized access attempts, leveraging system logs to quickly identify potential security breaches.

----

8. Fill in the blank: _____ is the primary tool used for identifying abnormal network traffic patterns that could indicate potential threats.

A: Network Monitoring Tools

B: Intrusion Detection System (IDS)

C: Traffic Flow Analysis

D: Firewall Log Analysis

Correct Answer: B

Explanation: An Intrusion Detection System (IDS) is crucial for identifying abnormal network traffic by analyzing traffic patterns and detecting anomalies that could suggest cyber threats, thereby playing a pivotal role in maintaining network security.

----

9. In a scenario where an organization's mobile devices are frequently lost, which technique would most effectively identify the risks associated with these incidents?

A: Increasing physical security measures in locations where devices are most often lost

B: Implementing a device tracking and management system for all company mobile devices

C: Requiring that all mobile devices be equipped with commercially available anti-theft devices

D: Conducting regular security training for employees on the importance of mobile security

Correct Answer: B

Explanation: Implementing a device tracking and management system is a strategic approach to mitigate the risks associated with lost mobile devices by enabling remote location tracking, device locking, or wiping to protect sensitive corporate data.

----

10. During a routine security audit, which technique should be employed first to identify potential security risks in a new software application?

A: Conducting a static code analysis using tools like SonarQube to evaluate the application's source code

B: Running a vulnerability scan on the application to identify known security flaws

C: Performing penetration testing to simulate real-world hacking attempts on the software

D: Reviewing user access logs to determine unusual patterns of behavior in the application

Correct Answer: A

Explanation: Conducting a static code analysis using tools like SonarQube allows for an in-depth review of new software applications' source code, identifying potential security vulnerabilities before the application is deployed or used in a production environment.

----

11. What command should be used to conduct an automated risk assessment of network services on a Linux server?

A: netcat -z -v 192.168.0.1 80

B: arp-scan --localnet

C: sudo nmap --script vuln 192.168.0.1

D: nessus -x 192.168.0.1 -V

Correct Answer: C

Explanation: The command sudo nmap --script vuln 192.168.0.1 initiates an Nmap vulnerability assessment, which automatically scans for known vulnerabilities on the specified IP address, providing crucial data for risk assessments by identifying potential security weaknesses.

----

12. In the context of a corporate IT system, which risk assessment method is most effective for determining the financial impact of potential data breaches?

A: Risk Matrix plotting

B: Cost-Benefit Analysis (CBA)

C: Qualitative Severity Assessment (QSA)

D: Annual Loss Expectancy (ALE) calculation

Correct Answer: D

Explanation: Annual Loss Expectancy (ALE) calculation is critical for quantifying the financial impact of potential data breaches by estimating the yearly cost of risks, which helps organizations prioritize their cybersecurity investments and mitigation strategies.

----

13. Fill in the blank: The use of _____ effectively determines the likelihood of future security incidents based on historical data.

A: Predictive analytics

B: Heuristic evaluation

C: Statistical inference

D: Trend analysis

Correct Answer: A

Explanation: Predictive analytics is instrumental in risk assessments as it utilizes historical incident data to forecast the likelihood and potential impact of future security threats, enabling proactive risk management and mitigation planning.

----

14. During an enterprise-wide risk assessment, which of the following strategies is essential for evaluating the impact of risks on business continuity?

A: Establishing a communication plan to notify stakeholders in the event of failure

B: Performing a Business Impact Analysis (BIA) for all critical systems

C: Drafting a risk response plan specific to each department's needs

D: Implementing redundant systems to automatically mitigate all identified risks

Correct Answer: B

Explanation: Conducting a Business Impact Analysis (BIA) is crucial for evaluating how different types of disruptions can affect critical business operations and for developing strategies that minimize the impact of risks on business continuity, ensuring that key business functions can continue during a crisis.

----

15. Considering an upcoming software upgrade, how should a cybersecurity technician assess the potential security risks associated with the new software version?

A: Conducting a full system backup before installing the new software version

B: Rolling out the software update to a small group of users as a pilot project

C: Testing the new software version in a controlled, isolated environment first

D: Reviewing the change logs and conducting a regression test on the upgraded software

Correct Answer: D

Explanation: Reviewing the change logs and conducting regression tests on the upgraded software ensures that new changes do not reintroduce old vulnerabilities or create new security risks, thus maintaining the integrity and security of the software environment after updates.

----

16. What command would you use to implement network segmentation as a risk mitigation strategy on a Cisco router?

A: config terminal; vlan 20; name Accounting; interface fa0/1; switchport access vlan 20

B: router rip; network 192.168.1.0; passive-interface default

C: interface range fa0/1 - 24; shutdown

D: ip access-list standard 10; permit 192.168.1.0 0.0.0.255

Correct Answer: A

Explanation: The command config terminal; vlan 20; name Accounting; interface fa0/1; switchport access vlan 20 correctly sets up a VLAN on a Cisco router, effectively segmenting the network which isolates network traffic and reduces the risk of lateral movement from potential cyber threats.

----

17. In addressing the risk of data breaches, which strategy effectively reduces risk exposure when employees use their personal devices for work?

A: Implementing a Mobile Device Management (MDM) solution with strict security policies

B: Requiring all personal devices to connect via a VPN when accessing corporate resources

C: Conducting periodic security audits of all personal devices used for work

D: Creating an isolated network for personal devices that cannot access sensitive information

Correct Answer: A

Explanation: Implementing a Mobile Device Management (MDM) solution with strict security policies allows for centralized control of security features on personal devices used for work, thus reducing the risk of data breaches by ensuring compliance with corporate security standards.

----

18. Fill in the blank: To mitigate the risk of unauthorized data access, administrators should enforce _____ on sensitive systems.

A: password expiration policies

B: least privilege access controls

C: regular security awareness seminars

D: multi-factor authentication (MFA)

Correct Answer: B

Explanation: Enforcing least privilege access controls ensures that users have access only to the resources they need for their job functions, thereby reducing the risk of unauthorized data access by limiting potential exposure points.

----

19. Considering an increase in phishing attacks, what risk mitigation strategy should be implemented to protect senior executives?

A: Installing advanced malware protection software on all executive devices

B: Limiting email access to work devices only

C: Monitoring email traffic for phishing attempts using AI-based tools

D: Providing tailored cybersecurity training focused on social engineering tactics

Correct Answer: D

Explanation: Providing tailored cybersecurity training focused on social engineering tactics specifically for senior executives helps mitigate the risk of phishing attacks by equipping them with the knowledge and skills to recognize and respond appropriately to such threats.

----

20. Which configuration should be applied to strengthen the security posture of a public-facing web server?

A: Implementing a Web Application Firewall (WAF) to detect and block malicious requests

B: Encrypting all data stored on the server using AES 256-bit encryption

C: Setting HTTP security headers and enabling HSTS on the server

D: Disabling unused services and closing unnecessary ports on the server

Correct Answer: C

Explanation: Setting HTTP security headers and enabling HTTP Strict Transport Security (HSTS) on a public-facing web server mitigates risks by enforcing secure connections and reducing the risk of man-in-the-middle attacks and other web-based threats.

----

21. What command can be used to set up continuous monitoring of HTTP traffic on a Linux server using Tcpdump?

A: sudo wireshark -k -i eth0 -f 'port 80' -w /tmp/http_capture.pcap

B: sudo snort -i eth0 -c /etc/snort/snort.conf -A console

C: sudo ngrep -d eth0 'HTTP' -O /tmp/http_capture.pcap

D: sudo tcpdump -i eth0 'tcp port 80' -w /var/log/http_traffic.log

Correct Answer: D

Explanation: Using sudo tcpdump -i eth0 'tcp port 80' -w /var/log/http_traffic.log enables continuous monitoring of HTTP traffic, capturing all data on port 80 and writing it to a log file, which is essential for identifying and responding to potential web-based threats in real-time.

----

22. How should a security team configure a SIEM tool for effective real-time monitoring of an organization's network security posture?

A: Configuring alerts for unusual outbound traffic patterns and failed login attempts

B: Running quarterly network penetration tests and annual security training for employees

C: Setting up daily security log reviews and monthly compliance assessments

D: Utilizing automated patch management systems to update firewall and antivirus software

Correct Answer: A

Explanation: Configuring a SIEM tool to alert on unusual outbound traffic and failed login attempts allows for immediate detection and response to potential security incidents, ensuring that the organization's network security posture is continuously monitored and maintained.

----

23. Fill in the blank: To continuously monitor for unauthorized access, system logs should be configured to trigger alerts for _____.

A: irregular file deletion events

B: repeated password reset requests

C: multiple failed login attempts

D: unusual application installation activities

Correct Answer: C

Explanation: Setting system logs to trigger alerts for multiple failed login attempts is a critical measure for monitoring unauthorized access attempts, providing real-time alerts that enable swift action to prevent potential breaches.

----

24. In a scenario where an organization's database has been experiencing irregular access patterns, what is the best initial step for continuous risk monitoring?

A: Implementing real-time database access monitoring and anomaly detection tools

B: Scheduling weekly database access audits to review access logs and user activities

C: Creating a task force to investigate each incident of irregular database access manually

D: Updating database security protocols and changing administrator passwords

Correct Answer: A

Explanation: Implementing real-time monitoring and anomaly detection tools for database access helps in immediately identifying and responding to irregular access patterns, thereby effectively monitoring ongoing risks and enhancing database security.

----

25. What configuration should be applied to ensure continuous security monitoring of remote workstation access within a corporate network?

A: Deploying network access control (NAC) solutions that monitor and enforce compliance policies on all devices

B: Setting up a virtual private network (VPN) for remote workstations with encrypted communication

C: Installing antivirus software on all remote workstations and scheduling daily scans

D: Implementing biometric authentication for all remote workstation users to enhance security

Correct Answer: A

Explanation: Deploying Network Access Control (NAC) solutions ensures continuous monitoring of all devices accessing the corporate network, enforcing compliance with security policies, and mitigating risks associated with remote workstation access.

----

26. What configuration command on a Cisco firewall ensures GDPR compliance by restricting data flow to specified geographic regions?

A: crypto map GDPR_MAP 10 ipsec-isakmp dynamic GDPR_DYNAMIC

B: route-map GDPR_ROUTE permit 10 set ip next-hop 192.0.2.1

C: ip access-list extended GDPR_Compliance permit ip any host 192.168.10.0 eq 443 deny ip any any

D: access-group GDPR_Filter in interface outside deny ip any host 203.0.113.0

Explanation: The command ip access-list extended GDPR_Compliance permit ip any host 192.168.10.0 eq 443 deny ip any any sets up an access control list on a Cisco firewall that restricts data traffic to a specified geographic region, which is crucial for GDPR compliance by ensuring that data does not leave the EU without proper safeguards.

----

27. When configuring a database that contains PHI for HIPAA compliance, which encryption method should be utilized?

A: Using MD5 hashing for password protection in the database

B: Implementing RSA 2048-bit encryption on database backups only

C: Transparent Data Encryption (TDE) on all tables storing PHI

D: Applying AES-256 encryption to data in transit only

Explanation: Implementing Transparent Data Encryption (TDE) on all tables storing PHI is crucial for HIPAA compliance as it encrypts sensitive data at rest, thereby protecting it against unauthorized access and data breaches.

----

28. Fill in the blank: To adhere to SOX compliance, system logs must be retained for a minimum duration of _____.

A: five years

B: three years

C: seven years

D: ten years

Explanation: Retaining system logs for a minimum of seven years is a requirement under SOX compliance to ensure that financial data and associated logs are available for audit purposes, which helps in maintaining transparency and accountability.

----

29. In preparing for a PCI DSS audit, what is the first step a cybersecurity technician should take regarding data storage systems?

A: Implementing additional firewall rules to restrict access to the cardholder data environment

B: Conducting a comprehensive review of all stored payment card data to ensure it's encrypted

C: Updating all server software to the latest versions to patch known vulnerabilities

D: Scheduling quarterly risk assessments to identify vulnerabilities in the data storage systems

Correct Answer: B

Explanation: Conducting a comprehensive review of all stored payment card data to ensure it's encrypted is the first and most critical step in preparing for a PCI DSS audit, as it addresses the primary concern of securing cardholder data against unauthorized access.

----

30. What GDPR compliance measure should be implemented on a web server to ensure that all personal data requests are logged and auditable?

A: Configuring server logging to include detailed access logs, user actions, and timestamps

B: Disabling all unnecessary services and ports on the server

C: Enabling gzip compression on all data transfers to and from the server

D: Implementing a Content Security Policy header to prevent cross-site scripting attacks

Correct Answer: A

Explanation: Configuring server logging to include detailed access logs, user actions, and timestamps is vital for GDPR compliance, as it ensures that all requests for personal data are logged and auditable, supporting transparency and accountability in data processing activities.

----

31. How should you configure an SIEM tool to ensure it aligns with a company's cybersecurity policy under the ISO/IEC 27001 framework?

A: Program the SIEM to focus solely on detecting malware infections and ransomware attacks

B: Set SIEM to generate alerts for unauthorized access attempts and non-compliance with established policies

C: Schedule monthly compliance reports that assess alignment with internal standards

D: Configure the SIEM to archive all logs bi-annually regardless of content or context

Explanation: Setting the SIEM to generate alerts for unauthorized access and policy non-compliance ensures that the system aligns with ISO/IEC 27001's requirements for continual monitoring and improvement of the information security management system, enhancing overall security posture and compliance.

----

32. Which command enforces a password complexity policy in a Windows environment to align with the NIST Cybersecurity Framework?

A: Set local security policy via gpedit.msc to enforce user account lockouts after three failed attempts

B: Apply a registry hack to disable USB ports to prevent physical data breaches

C: net accounts /minpwlen:12 /minpwage:7 /maxpwage:30

D: Use secpol.msc to disable guest accounts and enforce password expiration policies

Explanation: The command net accounts /minpwlen:12 /minpwage:7 /maxpwage:30 sets minimum and maximum password ages and a minimum password length, directly supporting the password management requirements of the NIST Cybersecurity Framework by enforcing strong password policies.

----

33. Fill in the blank: A critical step in aligning IT systems with the COBIT framework is ensuring that audit logs are _____.

A: periodically reviewed and backed up to an external drive

B: continuously monitored and retained for at least five years

C: occasionally checked during quarterly IT audits

D: securely encrypted and only accessible to department heads

Explanation: Ensuring that audit logs are continuously monitored and retained for at least five years aligns with COBIT's focus on regulatory compliance and risk management, providing necessary records to support audits and reviews.

----

34. What initial setup should be done on a network firewall to comply with the CIS Controls framework for small to medium enterprises?

A: Enabling deep packet inspection on all inbound and outbound traffic

B: Configuring access control lists to limit data flows strictly to essential services

C: Setting up geolocation blocking to prevent access from high-risk countries

D: Installing a web application firewall to monitor for SQL injection and XSS attacks

Correct Answer: B
Explanation: Configuring access control lists to strictly limit data flows to essential services is a fundamental setup under the CIS Controls, focusing on the principle of least privilege, which is crucial for securing SME network environments against unnecessary exposures.

----

35. For a company following the ITIL framework, what is the best practice for handling incidents that could affect security policies?

A: Implementing a structured process for logging, categorizing, and responding to incidents

B: Assigning a designated team to manually monitor and address incidents as they occur

C: Using an automated tool to detect and resolve incidents without human intervention

D: Encouraging employees to report incidents via an informal, verbal process to their supervisors

Correct Answer: A
Explanation: Implementing a structured process for logging, categorizing, and responding to incidents as per ITIL best practices ensures that incidents are managed systematically and efficiently, enhancing the organization's capability to respond to and recover from incidents, thereby maintaining security and service continuity.

----

36. In a large organization, a security analyst is tasked with auditing the security policy concerning user authentication and access controls. The analyst must review a Linux server's configuration to verify compliance with the policy. Which command should the analyst execute to review user password policies?

A: cat /etc/shadow

B: sudo grep '^PASS_' /etc/login.defs

C: sudo passwd -S

D: ls -la /etc/passwd

Explanation: This command correctly identifies the lines in the login.defs file that start with 'PASS_', which contain the password policies such as minimum length and expiration time. This is essential for verifying that the user password policies on a Linux server comply with the organization's security policies.

----

37. As part of an annual review, a company's cybersecurity team needs to ensure that their firewall configurations align with the latest security policies. What command should be used to display the current ruleset on a Cisco ASA firewall?

A: display current-configuration

B: show access-list

C: inspect firewall

D: show running-config

Explanation: show access-list' is the correct command to view all active access control lists on a Cisco ASA firewall, allowing the analyst to verify whether the firewall rules align with the current security policies.

----

38. Fill in the blank: To enforce password complexity rules across a Windows network, an IT administrator should update the _____ policy to include password length and complexity requirements.

A: Account Policies

B: Local Security Policy

C: Security Templates

D: Group Policy Object

Explanation: The Group Policy Object (GPO) in Windows Active Directory environments is used to manage various security and user policies, including password policies. Updating the GPO to set password complexity requirements ensures that all user accounts adhere to the organization's security standards.

---

39. A security manager is creating a new security policy for data encryption. The policy mandates that any data at rest within the company's cloud storage must be encrypted using a minimum of AES-256 encryption. The team is evaluating different cloud service providers. What should be the primary focus of their security assessment questionnaire?

A: The certifications of the cloud provider

B: The redundancy of network infrastructure

C: The physical security measures at data centers

D: The level of encryption provided for data at rest

Correct Answer: D

Explanation: When assessing cloud service providers for data encryption policies, the primary concern should be the encryption level offered for data at rest, ensuring it meets the company's minimum requirement of AES-256 encryption, as stated in the new security policy.

---

40. An organization is implementing a new security policy that requires logging all administrative actions on network devices. The IT team is tasked with configuring a Cisco router to ensure compliance. Which configuration command should they use to enable logging of all commands executed in privileged mode?

A: enable secret logging synchronous

B: terminal monitor

C: show running-config | include log

D: configuration terminal

Correct Answer: A

Explanation: The command 'enable secret logging synchronous' is used to configure a Cisco router to log all commands executed in privileged mode, ensuring that all administrative actions are tracked and logged, in compliance with the organization's new security policy.

---

41. A cybersecurity technician needs to configure a syslog server to collect logs from multiple devices for monitoring and accountability purposes. Which protocol and port number should the technician ensure are open to receive logs securely?

A: Syslog over TLS, port 6514

B: FTP, port 21

C: HTTP, port 80

D: SNMPv3, port 161

Correct Answer: A

Explanation: Using Syslog over TLS on port 6514 ensures that log data is transmitted securely between devices and the syslog server, protecting against unauthorized access and ensuring the integrity of the logs, which is crucial for accurate monitoring and accountability in security operations.

---

42. In an incident response scenario, a security analyst wants to verify the integrity of log files to ensure they have not been tampered with. Which hashing algorithm is most suitable for verifying the integrity of these files?

A: CRC32

B: MD5

C: SHA-256

D: SHA-1

Correct Answer: C

Explanation: SHA-256 is a cryptographic hash function that provides a high level of security and is resistant to collision attacks, making it highly suitable for verifying the integrity of log files, as it ensures that any alteration of the log data can be detected.

---

43. Fill in the blank: To set up an audit trail that captures all successful and failed login attempts on a server, the administrator must configure the _____ daemon.

A: syslogd

B: auditd

C: sshd

D: crond

Correct Answer: B
Explanation: The auditd daemon is specifically designed for auditing on Linux systems. It tracks security-relevant information, recording details about system calls, file accesses, and system logins, including both successful and unsuccessful attempts, thereby providing a comprehensive audit trail.

----

44. During a security audit, the auditor finds that logs from network devices are not being retained long enough to meet regulatory requirements. What is the best initial action the auditor should recommend to address this issue?
A: Conduct a follow-up audit in one month

B: Review and modify the log retention policy

C: Immediately cease use of current devices

D: Increase storage capacity on the logging server

Correct Answer: B
Explanation: Reviewing and modifying the log retention policy is the most direct and effective way to address issues with log retention times. This ensures that the organization's logging practices are aligned with regulatory requirements and that logs are available for review in the event of an audit or security incident.

----

45. A company's security policy requires that all administrative accesses to the switches be logged and reviewed monthly. What configuration command should be used on a Cisco switch to enable logging of all level 15 (privileged EXEC mode) command executions?
A: enable secret logging level 15

B: logging buffer-size 50000

C: archive log config logging enable

D: configure terminal logging enable

Correct Answer: C
Explanation: The command 'archive log config logging enable' is used on Cisco switches to log all commands executed in privileged EXEC mode, ensuring that all administrative

accesses are recorded. This allows for periodic reviews and audits, satisfying company policy requirements for accountability and oversight of switch management.

----

46. A company is assessing its IT infrastructure to ensure high availability. Which configuration would provide the highest level of redundancy for their data center servers?

A: Dual power supplies, RAID 5 storage, and multiple network paths

B: Single power supply, RAID 0 storage, one network path

C: Single UPS, single power source, RAID 1 storage

D: Multiple UPS, RAID 10 storage, dual network paths

Correct Answer: A

Explanation: The combination of dual power supplies, RAID 5 storage, and multiple network paths provides the best redundancy and fault tolerance, ensuring that server operations can continue even if one component fails. This setup minimizes downtime and data loss, which is essential for maintaining business operations during unexpected disruptions.

----

47. During a risk assessment, a cybersecurity manager must evaluate the effectiveness of business continuity plans. Which type of test involves a full-scale simulation of a disaster scenario to validate the plan?

A: Full interruption test

B: Walk-through test

C: Paper test

D: Tabletop exercise

Correct Answer: A

Explanation: A full interruption test involves a complete shutdown of operations at the primary site and a switch to the disaster recovery site, simulating a real disaster scenario. This test is crucial for validating the effectiveness of the business continuity plan, ensuring that all processes and infrastructures perform as expected in an emergency.

----

48. Fill in the blank: For a critical application server, the configuration file ____ should be regularly backed up to a secure, offsite location to ensure business continuity.

A: /etc/application.conf

B: /etc/backup.conf

C: /var/run/app.pid

D: /usr/local/etc/config.xml

Correct Answer: A

Explanation: Regular backups of the /etc/application.conf file are essential for recovery operations because this file typically contains critical configuration settings for applications. Ensuring it is stored offsite protects against data loss during physical disasters at the primary site, thereby supporting continuity of operations.

----

49. A financial institution is implementing a disaster recovery plan that includes setting up a hot site. What is the most critical factor when configuring the network at the hot site?

A: Cost-effectiveness of the hot site solutions

B: Synchronization of data replication between primary and hot sites

C: Physical security measures at the hot site

D: The distance between the hot site and the primary site

Correct Answer: B

Explanation: Synchronization of data replication is vital when configuring a network at a hot site because it ensures that the backup location always has the most current data. This allows the business to continue operations with minimal disruption in the event of a disaster at the primary site.

----

50. Following a regional power outage, a data center's operations were disrupted. What command should be used on a Linux server to immediately start an automated script for system shutdown and failover to a backup data center?

A: /sbin/shutdown -r now

B: /bin/bash failover-script.sh

C: systemctl restart network.service

D: echo "shutdown" | /sbin/poweroff

Correct Answer: A

Explanation: The command '/sbin/shutdown -r now' is used on Linux servers to perform an immediate reboot. In the context of a power outage and the need for a quick failover, this command can trigger an automated shutdown script that includes failover procedures to a backup data center, thus ensuring continuity of services.

----

51. In configuring a server to ensure data redundancy as part of a disaster recovery plan, which RAID configuration provides fault tolerance and data mirroring?

A: RAID 5

B: RAID 0

C: RAID 1

D: RAID 10

Correct Answer: C

Explanation: RAID 1 creates an exact copy (or mirror) of a set of data on two or more disks. This is a straightforward method to achieve data mirroring and fault tolerance, which are essential components of a robust disaster recovery plan as they allow for continuous data availability and minimal downtime in the event of hardware failure.

----

52. To verify the backup integrity of critical data, which command should a technician use on a UNIX system to check the checksum of a file?

A: sha256sum filename.tar.gz

B: tar -tzf filename.tar.gz

C: ls -l filename.tar.gz

D: cksum filename.tar.gz

Correct Answer: D

Explanation: The cksum command in UNIX is used to calculate the checksum of files to verify their integrity. This command is crucial for confirming that a backup file has not been corrupted or altered, which is critical to ensure the reliability of data backups.

----

53. Fill in the blank: To automate the backup process on a Windows Server, the system administrator should schedule backups using the _____ tool.

A: Task Scheduler

B: Control Panel

C: Windows Server Backup

D: Command Prompt

Correct Answer: C

Explanation: Windows Server Backup is an integrated tool in Windows Server that allows administrators to schedule automatic backups. This feature is vital for implementing consistent backup routines, ensuring that all critical data is preserved regularly without manual intervention, which supports disaster recovery strategies.

----

54. A team is drafting a disaster recovery plan for a newly deployed application that includes an SQL database. What is the most crucial aspect to include in the plan to ensure data recovery for this specific application?

A: A detailed process for SQL database replication and recovery

B: Steps to change application configuration settings after recovery

C: Guidelines on regular software updates and patch management

D: Instructions for reinstalling the application from scratch

Correct Answer: A

Explanation: Including a detailed process for SQL database replication and recovery in a disaster recovery plan is essential for applications dependent on database integrity and availability. This process ensures that the database can be quickly restored to its last consistent state, minimizing data loss and downtime.

----

55. After experiencing a data breach, a company needs to restore its systems from backups. Which PowerShell command should be used to initiate the restoration process of the system state from a backup?

A: Get-WBBackupSet -BackupSetIdentifier $id

B: Set-WBRecovery -BackupSetIdentifier $id

C: Restore-WBFile -BackupSetIdentifier $id

D: Start-WBSystemStateRecovery -BackupSetIdentifier $id

Correct Answer: D

Explanation: The PowerShell command Start-WBSystemStateRecovery is used to begin the system state recovery from a specified backup set. This is critical for restoring a system to a previous state following a disaster, such as a data breach, and is particularly useful in quickly re-establishing the operational status of critical servers and services.

----

56. A network administrator is setting up an automated backup solution for a company's financial databases. Which command should be used to perform a full backup using rsync over SSH for secure data transfer?

A: rsync -avz -e ssh /source/dir username@remote:/dest/dir

B: rsync -a /source/dir /dest/dir

C: ssh username@remote "cat > /dest/dir" < /source/dir/tar.gz

D: scp -r /source/dir username@remote:/dest/dir

Correct Answer: A

Explanation: The command rsync -avz -e ssh /source/dir username@remote:/dest/dir is used to securely backup data over the internet using SSH for encryption. The flags -avz ensure that the data is transferred in archive mode, which preserves symbolic links, permissions, and timestamps, and -z compresses the data to speed up the transfer.

----

57. To ensure data integrity, which command is most appropriate for verifying that a backup file has not been altered after its creation on a Linux system?

A: sha256sum -c backupfile.sha256

B: diff -u originalfile backupfile

C: md5sum -c backupfile.md5

D: cksum backupfile

Correct Answer: A

Explanation: The sha256sum -c backupfile.sha256 command is used to check the integrity of the backup file by comparing the current checksum of the backup file to the original checksum stored in backupfile.sha256. This command is critical for ensuring that the backup file has not been tampered with or corrupted.

----

58. Fill in the blank: To automate data backups on a Linux system, a system administrator can use the _____ utility, which is commonly used for scheduling tasks including backups.

A: cron

B: at

C: anacron

D: systemctl

Explanation: The cron utility is used on Linux systems to schedule tasks to run at specified times. It is ideal for setting up regular automated backups, ensuring that critical data is backed up systematically without manual intervention.

----

59. When planning to backup a server's data to a remote location, what is the primary consideration to ensure data recovery capabilities in a disaster recovery scenario?

A: Physical accessibility of the remote site

B: Reliability and speed of the network connection to the remote site

C: Cost of storage at the remote site

D: Security of the data at the remote location

Explanation: The primary consideration when backing up data to a remote location should be the reliability and speed of the network connection to the remote site, as this directly affects the ability to quickly and reliably access or restore the backup data in the event of a disaster.

----

60. A system administrator needs to restore a corrupted directory from a backup archive using tar. Which command should they use to correctly restore the directory while preserving file permissions?

A: tar -xzvf backup.tar.gz -C /restore/path

B: tar -xvpzf backup.tar.gz -C /restore/path

C: restore -x /restore/path < backup.tar

D: unzip backup.zip -d /restore/path

Explanation: The command tar -xvpzf backup.tar.gz -C /restore/path is used to extract a tar archived backup while preserving file permissions. The -xvpzf options ensure that tar extracts the files, preserves permissions, and handles the gzip decompression, making it the correct choice for restoring data accurately from a backup archive.

----

61. Which command should be used on a Linux system to encrypt a directory using GnuPG, thereby preventing unauthorized access to sensitive data within it?

A: zip -P password mydirectory.zip mydirectory/*

B: openssl enc -aes-256-cbc -in mydirectory.tar.gz -out mydirectory.enc

C: tar -zcvf mydirectory.tar.gz | openssl enc -aes-256-cbc -out mydirectory.enc

D: gpg -c --batch --passphrase-file /my/pwfile mydirectory.tar.gz

Correct Answer: D

Explanation: The command gpg -c --batch --passphrase-file /my/pwfile mydirectory.tar.gz is used for encrypting files or directories with GnuPG, providing a secure method to ensure data confidentiality. The use of a passphrase file in batch mode ensures that encryption can be automated securely without manual passphrase entry, which is crucial for maintaining the integrity and confidentiality of sensitive data.

\---

62. In a Windows environment, what policy should be configured to prevent unauthorized external devices from accessing sensitive data?

A: Device Installation Restrictions

B: BitLocker Drive Encryption

C: User Account Control settings

D: Firewall Settings

Correct Answer: A

Explanation: Device Installation Restrictions policy in Windows environments is crucial for preventing unauthorized devices from accessing sensitive data. By controlling which devices can be installed, organizations can mitigate the risk of data leakage through unauthorized or insecure devices.

\---

63. Fill in the blank: To monitor and block sensitive data from being sent via email, configure _____ rules in the company's email gateway.

A: anti-spam

B: content filtering

C: malware scanning

D: attachment control

Correct Answer: B

Explanation: Configuring content filtering rules in an email gateway is an effective measure to monitor and prevent sensitive data from being sent outside the organization. These rules can inspect outgoing emails for sensitive information and block them if necessary, thus enforcing data loss prevention policies.

----

64. When deploying a DLP solution in a corporate network, what is the primary feature to look for in order to prevent unauthorized access to sensitive files stored on network drives?

A: Real-time monitoring and alerts for file access attempts

B: Periodic vulnerability scans of file servers

C: Encrypted storage of all network files

D: Use of strong file permissions

Correct Answer: A

Explanation: The feature of real-time monitoring and alerts for file access attempts is essential in a DLP solution for network drives. It allows for immediate detection and response to unauthorized access attempts, helping to prevent data breaches and ensuring compliance with data protection policies.

----

65. A security administrator is setting up network access control (NAC) to restrict access to the corporate network based on the compliance of the connecting device with the company's security policies. Which protocol is best suited for implementing this control?

A: SNMPv3

B: RADIUS

C: IEEE 802.1X

D: IPsec

Correct Answer: C

Explanation: IEEE 802.1X is the best protocol for implementing network access control (NAC) as it provides an authentication mechanism to devices trying to connect to a network. This protocol helps ensure that only compliant and authorized devices can access network resources, thereby enhancing the security posture of an organization.

----

66. When configuring a logging system on a company server to ensure adherence to legal and ethical standards, which log level should be prioritized to capture potential illegal access without causing personal privacy concerns?

A: Configure logs to rotate and archive every 24 hours, regardless of log level, to balance system performance with monitoring needs.

B: Record all log levels, including Debug and Information, to ensure comprehensive monitoring of all activities on the server.

C: Store only Error and Critical log levels to prevent over-collection of data that might include user personal information.

D: Include Information, Warning, and Critical log levels but exclude Debug to minimize the volume of logged data.

Correct Answer: C

Explanation: Prioritizing Error and Critical log levels helps in capturing significant security events while respecting user privacy by not over-collecting data, thus aligning with both ethical guidelines and legal standards regarding personal data protection.

----

67. In drafting a policy for ethical hacking within a company, what should be the primary guideline for the scope of allowed activities?

A: Ethical hacking should be restricted to non-production environments to eliminate risks to business operations.

B: Hacking activities should primarily focus on externally facing systems to prevent internal disruptions and maintain focus on potential entry points.

C: The activities must only target systems for which explicit permission has been obtained from the system owners and documented.

D: Hacking activities can be carried out on any system without prior notification to understand the real-world scenario of an attack.

Correct Answer: C

Explanation: By ensuring hacking activities only target systems with documented permission from owners, the policy adheres to ethical hacking principles, protecting both the organization's integrity and legal standing by preventing unauthorized access.

----

68. Given the command chmod 700 /var/log/audit.log, explain the legality of this permission setting in terms of user privacy and data protection.

A: This command sets the file as readable, writable, and executable by anyone, raising significant concerns about data security and user privacy.

B: This command removes all special permissions, making the audit log file potentially accessible to unauthorized users, which could lead to legal issues.

C: The permission setting is too restrictive and may hinder audits and monitoring processes that require broader access by authorized personnel.

D: This setting ensures that only the root user can access the log file, limiting access to sensitive data and adhering to the principle of least privilege.

Correct Answer: D

Explanation: Setting chmod 700 for /var/log/audit.log limits access to this sensitive log file to the root user only, thereby enforcing data security through the principle of least privilege, which is crucial for complying with legal and ethical standards concerning access to personal and confidential information.

----

69. An incident response team receives a directive to decrypt employee emails as part of a legal investigation. What should be their first step to ensure this action complies with both legal and ethical standards?

A: Verify the request's legality with the company's legal counsel to ensure it aligns with privacy laws and company policies before proceeding.

B: Seek employee consent before proceeding with decryption, regardless of the investigation's nature.

C: Start decrypting emails after informing all employees about the investigation to maintain transparency.

D: Immediately decrypt the emails as requested, assuming the directive comes from a trusted authority.

Correct Answer: A

Explanation: Consulting legal counsel before decrypting employee emails ensures that the response team adheres to legal requirements and ethical standards, prioritizing the protection of employee privacy and the organization's compliance with applicable laws.

----

70. A company implements an intrusion detection system (IDS). What is the primary ethical concern to address in the IDS configuration to avoid potential legal issues?

A: Integrate the IDS with external threat intelligence services to enhance detection without addressing ethical or legal implications.

B: Set the IDS to monitor and store all network traffic, including payload data, to ensure thorough analysis and detection capabilities.

C: Adjust the IDS settings to perform deep packet inspection on all data to ensure maximum security and detection capabilities.

D: Configure the IDS to disregard packet payload content, focusing instead on header data to respect privacy and comply with data protection laws.

Correct Answer: D
Explanation: By configuring the IDS to avoid analyzing packet payload, the system focuses on metadata which reduces the risk of violating privacy rights and ensures compliance with data protection laws, addressing the primary ethical concern of unnecessary invasion of privacy while maintaining security monitoring capabilities.

----

71. What command should be used to audit the firewall rules that apply to traffic from third-party vendor IPs to ensure compliance with your organization's security policy?

A: Execute sudo iptables -L | grep -i 'vendor IP' to list active rules affecting specified vendor IPs.

B: Run traceroute 'vendor IP' to see the path packets take from vendors to your network.

C: Apply ping 'vendor IP' to check the availability and response time from the vendor's network.

D: Use netstat -an | grep 'vendor IP' to monitor all current connections from vendor IPs.

Correct Answer: A
Explanation: Using sudo iptables -L | grep -i 'vendor IP' allows administrators to view specific firewall rules affecting traffic from third-party vendor IPs, ensuring that all traffic complies with organizational security policies by verifying that only authorized communications are allowed.

----

72. In a contract with a new software vendor, which clause is crucial for protecting your company data from unauthorized third-party access?

A: Stipulate that any breach involving vendor access must be reported within 24 hours.

B: Require an annual security audit report from the vendor, detailing their compliance with industry standards.

C: Include a Data Protection Agreement that specifies encryption standards and access controls.

D: Mandate that the vendor uses only pre-approved software and hardware while accessing company data.

Correct Answer: C

Explanation: Incorporating a Data Protection Agreement with specified encryption standards and access controls into contracts with software vendors is crucial to ensure that sensitive company data is handled securely and in accordance with best practices, thereby protecting the data from unauthorized third-party access.

----

73. Fill in the blank: To track and verify the integrity of files exchanged with third-party vendors, use the Linux command _____.

A: chkconfig

B: ls -l

C: sha256sum

D: md5sum

Correct Answer: C

Explanation: The sha256sum command is used to compute and verify the SHA-256 hash of files, making it an excellent tool for tracking and ensuring the integrity of files exchanged with vendors by providing a means to detect any unauthorized changes to the files.

----

74. During a security review, you identify that a vendor's access to your network is overly broad. What's the first action to take in response?

A: Evaluate the current access permissions and implement the principle of least privilege by restricting their access to only what is necessary.

B: Request the vendor to provide a detailed justification for the need for broad network access.

C: Increase the security of the network by enhancing encryption methods and security protocols.

D: Directly cut off all network access for the vendor until a thorough risk assessment is completed.

Correct Answer: A

Explanation: Evaluating and then implementing the principle of least privilege for vendor access ensures that vendors have only the necessary permissions to fulfill their tasks, which minimizes potential security risks by reducing the access points available for exploitation.

----

75. A scenario involves a vendor who needs to access a protected database. What should be the initial step to secure this access?
A: Establish a VPN with multi-factor authentication for the vendor before granting database access.

B: Require the vendor to install proprietary security software developed by your company.

C: Create an isolated subnet for the vendor without additional security measures.

D: Grant direct database access but monitor the vendor's activities through detailed logging.

Correct Answer: A

Explanation: Setting up a VPN with multi-factor authentication as an initial step provides a secure, encrypted channel for the vendor to access the necessary database, effectively safeguarding sensitive data by adding an essential layer of security that helps prevent unauthorized access.

----

76. Which command should be used to verify the digital signature of a software package to ensure it has not been tampered with by a supply chain intermediary?
A: Run md5sum filename to quickly check if the file matches the original version provided by the supplier.

B: Execute chkconfig --list | grep software-name to review if the software is configured to start automatically.

C: Apply sha256sum filename | check against provided hash to ensure file integrity without verifying the source.

D: Use gpg --verify filename.sig filename to check the integrity and authenticity of the file.

Correct Answer: D

Explanation: Using gpg --verify filename.sig filename ensures that the software package received has not been altered from its original state by verifying its digital signature against the public key provided by the legitimate source. This command confirms both the integrity and the authenticity of the software, crucial for maintaining supply chain security.

----

77. What is the primary security measure to implement when integrating a new hardware component from a supplier into your network?

A: Physically inspect the hardware for any tampering signs before installation.

B: Conduct a security audit of the hardware, including firmware version checks and vulnerability scans.

C: Install a network firewall configured specifically to monitor the new hardware's traffic.

D: Update the network's antivirus software to the latest version before integrating the new hardware.

Correct Answer: B

Explanation: Conducting a security audit on new hardware components involves checking for the latest firmware versions and running vulnerability scans to identify any security weaknesses before the hardware is integrated into the network. This step is essential to prevent potential security breaches that could originate from compromised hardware components.

----

78. Fill in the blank: To ensure continuous security validation of software supplied by external vendors, integrate _____ into your CI/CD pipeline.

A: continuous integration service

B: automated security scanning tools

C: real-time compliance reporting

D: version control monitoring

Correct Answer: B

Explanation: Integrating automated security scanning tools into the Continuous Integration/Continuous Deployment (CI/CD) pipeline allows for continuous security validation of software. These tools automatically scan the software for vulnerabilities as it passes through stages of development and deployment, ensuring that security is maintained throughout the software lifecycle.

----

79. Given a scenario where a supplier's compromised system could threaten your data integrity, what is the first step in your incident response?

A: Review recent access logs to identify any unauthorized entries or suspicious activities.

B: Contact the supplier immediately to request a detailed report on their security breach.

C: Isolate the affected systems and begin a forensic analysis to determine the extent of the intrusion.

D: Update all system passwords and security protocols as a precautionary measure.

Correct Answer: C
Explanation: Isolating affected systems and conducting forensic analysis as the initial step in incident response to a supplier's compromised system helps contain the threat and understand how the breach occurred. This information is critical to prevent future incidents and to remediate current vulnerabilities effectively.

----

80. Your company plans to procure a network management system from a new vendor. What critical step must be performed before deployment?

A: Perform a comprehensive security assessment of the vendor, including past security incidents and current compliance statuses.

B: Implement an employee training program on the operational features and security practices related to the new system.

C: Require the vendor to provide financial compensation for potential security breaches as a contract clause.

D: Install the system in a test environment to monitor its performance and detect possible issues.

Correct Answer: A
Explanation: Performing a comprehensive security assessment of a new vendor includes investigating their past security incidents and assessing their compliance with relevant security standards. This step ensures that the vendor's security practices meet your organization's requirements, thereby mitigating risks associated with integrating their systems into your environment.

----

81. Which command is recommended for an employee to use to verify the security certificates of a website before entering sensitive information?

A: Run nslookup example.com to find out the IP address of the website.

B: Apply traceroute example.com to trace the path packets take to the host.

C: Use curl -Iv https://example.com to check SSL/TLS certificate details.

D: Execute ping example.com to see if the site is up before visiting it.

Correct Answer: C
Explanation: Using curl -Iv https://example.com allows employees to view detailed information about the SSL/TLS certificates of a website directly from their command line. This method ensures that the website they are accessing is secure and the certificate is valid, helping prevent entering sensitive information on compromised websites.

----

82. What should be the primary focus of a cybersecurity awareness training session for new employees?

A: Limit the training to updating antivirus software and managing firewall settings.

B: Focus exclusively on teaching how to use the company's VPN and other technical tools.

C: The main focus should be on compliance with industry-specific security regulations only.

D: Educate on recognizing phishing attempts and proper password management techniques.

Correct Answer: D
Explanation: Focusing on recognizing phishing attempts and proper password management techniques equips new employees with critical skills for protecting both personal and company data. These topics cover essential areas that are frequently targeted by cyber attackers, thus providing practical and immediately applicable knowledge.

----

83. Fill in the blank: To ensure secure password storage, it is recommended to hash passwords using the _____ algorithm.

A: bcrypt

B: aes-256

C: sha1

D: md5

Correct Answer: A
Explanation: The bcrypt algorithm is recommended for hashing passwords because it incorporates a salt to protect against rainbow table attacks and has a work factor that can

be adjusted to make it slower, thereby providing a strong defense against brute force attacks. This makes it an ideal choice for secure password storage.

----

84. In a training scenario, if an employee receives a suspicious email asking for their credentials, what is the first thing they should do?
A: Click on the link to confirm if the site looks legitimate or not.

B: Verify the sender's identity by cross-checking email addresses and contacting the supposed sender through official channels.

C: Forward the email to all colleagues to see if anyone else has received a similar message.

D: Ignore the email and assume the IT department will handle it if it's a serious threat.

Correct Answer: B
Explanation: Verifying the sender's identity by cross-checking email addresses and contacting the supposed sender through official channels ensures that the employee does not act on deceptive emails. This proactive step is crucial in preventing information leaks and maintaining the integrity of the company's communications.

----

85. A company conducts a drill simulating a phishing attack. What is the first step employees should take upon identifying the email as a phishing attempt?
A: Report the phishing attempt to the IT security team using the official reporting process.

B: Mark the email as spam to help the email system filter out similar messages in the future.

C: Respond to the phishing email to gather more information about the sender's intent.

D: Delete the email immediately to prevent any accidental clicks in the future.

Correct Answer: A
Explanation: Reporting the phishing attempt to the IT security team using the official reporting process is the correct first step in handling a simulated phishing attack. This action helps the security team track and mitigate potential threats, enhances the organization's response strategies, and fosters a proactive security culture among employees.

----

86. When assessing a cyber insurance policy, which tool can be used to calculate the potential financial impact of a data breach based on past incidents?

A: Implement the NIST Cybersecurity Framework as a holistic approach to managing all cybersecurity risks.

B: Use RiskLens software to specifically focus on qualitative risk analysis without considering financial metrics.

C: Apply the Cost of a Data Breach Report by Ponemon Institute to generalize expenses without company-specific input.

D: Utilize the FAIR (Factor Analysis of Information Risk) model to estimate and quantify risk exposure.

Correct Answer: D

Explanation: The FAIR model is a recognized and structured approach to quantifying and understanding the financial impacts of cybersecurity risks, making it ideal for assessing potential data breaches and supporting decisions related to cyber insurance policies.

\-

87. What critical factor should be considered when determining the limit of liability in a cyber insurance policy?

A: The total value of the data assets and potential revenue loss in the event of a cyber incident.

B: The age and technology dependency of the IT infrastructure, focusing on hardware vulnerability.

C: The number of employees, assuming more employees lead to a higher risk of accidental data exposure.

D: The geographical scope of the company's operations, including all countries where it is active.

Correct Answer: A

Explanation: Considering the total value of data assets and potential revenue loss in determining the limit of liability ensures that the cyber insurance coverage is adequate to cover the most significant financial impacts, providing a financial safety net that aligns with the company's risk exposure.

\-

88. **Fill in the blank: For proper record-keeping and to support potential cyber insurance claims, it is recommended to use the _____ tool for logging all network activity.**

A: Syslog

B: Wireshark

C: NetFlow

D: Snort

Correct Answer: A

Explanation: Using Syslog for logging all network activity ensures comprehensive and secure record-keeping that can be crucial for substantiating a cyber insurance claim following an incident. This tool captures detailed data about network behavior, which is invaluable during post-incident investigations and insurance assessments.

----

89. **In preparing for a cyber insurance audit, what is the first step to verify compliance with the terms of the insurance policy?**

A: Conduct a thorough review of all current cybersecurity measures and incident response plans.

B: Schedule a meeting with the company's financial department to discuss the impact of the current policy.

C: Immediately purchase additional coverage in areas where the current policy does not offer protection.

D: Start by renegotiating terms with the insurance provider to possibly include more favorable conditions.

Correct Answer: A

Explanation: Conducting a thorough review of all current cybersecurity measures and incident response plans as the first step in preparing for a cyber insurance audit helps ensure that the company's practices are in line with the terms of the insurance policy. This step is crucial for identifying any gaps or weaknesses that could affect compliance and coverage.

----

90. **A company wants to adjust its cyber insurance policy based on recent threat assessments. What should be the first step in this process?**

A: Expand the IT department to include more cybersecurity specialists and analysts to handle potential threats.

B: Increase the frequency of mandatory cybersecurity training sessions for all staff.

C: Review the latest security audit reports to align the insurance coverage with the identified risks.

D: Conduct an employee survey to gauge the general awareness and effectiveness of current security practices.

Correct Answer: C
Explanation: Reviewing the latest security audit reports as the first step in adjusting a cyber insurance policy ensures that the coverage adjustments are data-driven and based on the most recent and relevant threat information. This approach helps align the insurance policy with the current risk landscape, ensuring that coverage is neither insufficient nor excessively costly.

----

91. What command should be used to analyze network traffic in real-time to help identify potential threats as part of threat modeling?

A: Run nmap -O target_ip to perform OS detection and service scanning as part of threat evaluation.

B: Execute tcpdump -i eth0 not port 22 to capture and analyze packets excluding SSH traffic.

C: Apply wireshark to visually analyze traffic and capture data packets across the network.

D: Use netstat -tuln to list all open ports and listening services for understanding active connections.

Correct Answer: B
Explanation: Using tcpdump -i eth0 not port 22 allows for the monitoring of network traffic in real-time, excluding SSH traffic to reduce noise, making it easier to spot anomalies and potential threats. This command helps in understanding the data flow and spotting irregular patterns that may indicate cybersecurity threats.

----

92. In the context of software development, what is the most critical step to ensure during threat modeling for a new application?

A: Assign a dedicated team to perform post-deployment security monitoring without prior integration.

B: Integrating security reviews at each stage of the development lifecycle to identify vulnerabilities early.

C: Develop a single comprehensive threat model only after the entire application is developed.

D: Focusing solely on final stage testing to catch any last-minute issues before the application goes live.

Correct Answer: B

Explanation: Integrating security reviews at each development stage is crucial as it allows for the early detection and mitigation of security vulnerabilities within the application, thereby reducing the potential for exploitation and aligning with best practices in secure software development.

----

93. Fill in the blank: To assist in automated threat modeling, the use of _____ tools can help identify code vulnerabilities before deployment.

A: static analysis

B: dynamic scanning

C: risk mapping

D: penetration testing

Correct Answer: A

Explanation: Static analysis tools automate the process of code review to identify vulnerabilities before the application is deployed. These tools can effectively detect a wide range of common coding faults that can lead to security breaches, making them an essential part of threat modeling in software development.

----

94. If a threat model identifies a high-risk vulnerability in an organization's email system, what should be the initial response?

A: Send a company-wide alert to change passwords without assessing the specific vulnerability type.

B: Review and update the organization's incident response plan without addressing the vulnerability.

C: Immediately implement email filtering and security controls to mitigate the risk of phishing and malware.

D: Upgrade the email server software immediately to the latest version without a prior risk assessment.

Correct Answer: C

Explanation: Implementing email filtering and security controls immediately after identifying a high-risk vulnerability in the email system helps mitigate risks such as phishing and malware attacks. This response is proactive and focuses on preventing exploitation of the identified vulnerability, thereby enhancing the organization's resilience against email-based security threats.

----

95. A scenario involves a web application with potential SQL injection vulnerabilities. What preventive measure should be prioritized during threat modeling?

A: Apply strict firewall rules that block all SQL traffic to and from the web application server.

B: Implement parameterized queries or prepared statements in the application's database interactions.

C: Use encryption techniques on all data fields to prevent the extraction of meaningful information.

D: Require all users to change their passwords frequently to avoid potential unauthorized access.

Correct Answer: B
Explanation: Using parameterized queries or prepared statements is a direct and effective method to prevent SQL injection, which is a common vulnerability in web applications. This technique ensures that SQL queries are safe from injection attacks by separating the data from the code, thus enhancing the security of database interactions.

----

96. Which command helps verify the configuration and security settings of a Linux server to prepare for an audit?

A: Run sudo systemctl list-unit-files --type=service to review all service configurations and statuses.

B: Use chkconfig --list to see which legacy services are still active, without checking their security configurations.

C: Implement top to monitor real-time server performance, which does not provide direct audit compliance information.

D: Execute ps aux to list all running processes and manually check for any unusual activity.

Correct Answer: A
Explanation: Using sudo systemctl list-unit-files --type=service allows auditors to systematically review and confirm the configuration and operational status of all services on a Linux server, ensuring they are necessary, secure, and compliant with established

security policies. This command provides a comprehensive overview that is critical for a thorough audit.

----

97. What is an essential step to take before starting a security audit in an organization?

A: Start the audit unannounced to catch employees in their typical working state and potentially identify more issues.

B: Conduct an initial risk assessment using only external audit tools without internal stakeholder input.

C: Ensure all relevant stakeholders are informed about the audit scope and schedule to promote transparency and cooperation.

D: Skip preliminary meetings and directly engage with IT teams to start the technical evaluation phase.

Correct Answer: C
Explanation: Informing all relevant stakeholders about the audit's scope and schedule is crucial for ensuring organizational transparency and cooperation. This approach facilitates a smooth audit process, as stakeholders are prepared and can provide necessary information and access, thereby improving the audit's effectiveness and efficiency.

----

98. Fill in the blank: For tracking changes and ensuring compliance with configuration standards, the _____ utility is indispensable in security audits.

A: scp

B: rsync

C: cron

D: auditd

Correct Answer: D
Explanation: The auditd utility is fundamental for security audits as it provides detailed tracking of system activities by monitoring and logging system calls and file access. This utility helps ensure that changes and access are recorded, making it easier to verify compliance with security policies and standards.

----

99. During an audit, you discover unauthorized software on several company devices. What is the first action to take?

A: Immediately delete all unauthorized software found without investigating how it was installed or by whom.

B: Advise employees to avoid using the software without taking steps to remove it or assessing its impact.

C: Isolate the affected devices and conduct a thorough investigation to understand the extent of the potential compromise.

D: Update the antivirus software across all devices to detect any other potential threats immediately.

Correct Answer: C

Explanation: Isolating devices that contain unauthorized software and conducting a thorough investigation helps in understanding how the breach happened and the extent of the compromise. This is a critical first step in mitigating risk and preventing future security lapses.

----

100. A security audit reveals inadequate access controls on sensitive data. What is the first measure to implement?

A: Implement two-factor authentication for all users, regardless of the specifics of the access control issues.

B: Review and update user roles and permissions to ensure they adhere strictly to the principle of least privilege.

C: Increase network monitoring and logging without specifically addressing the access control flaws.

D: Mandate a company-wide password change immediately to prevent potential unauthorized data access.

Correct Answer: B

Explanation: Reviewing and updating user roles and permissions to adhere to the principle of least privilege is an essential measure following the discovery of inadequate access controls. This action directly addresses the core issue by restricting access to sensitive data only to those who legitimately need it, thereby enhancing the security posture.

----

101. A cybersecurity technician is analyzing traffic on their network and notices several outbound connections to unfamiliar IP addresses. Which of the following tools would most effectively allow them to capture and analyze this suspicious traffic?

A: Deploy an endpoint protection solution to block potentially harmful applications from executing.

B: Configure a web application firewall (WAF) to prevent common web-based attacks and unauthorized data leaks.

C: Set up a network performance monitor to assess bandwidth usage and identify potential bottlenecks.

D: Use a packet sniffer like Wireshark to capture and inspect the traffic for any data exfiltration or unauthorized commands.

Correct Answer: D

Explanation: Capturing and analyzing suspicious traffic is best achieved using a packet sniffer like Wireshark, which can detail the data being sent and received, helping to identify any unauthorized or malicious activity effectively.

----

102. In a security audit, a technician needs to verify if any changes were made to the firewall configuration that could expose internal services. What Unix command should they use to display the current firewall rules?

A: Apply tcpdump to capture and analyze traffic on the server for further investigation.

B: Run netstat -r to view routing tables and active connections on the network.

C: Use traceroute to map the path data takes to its destination, identifying any unexpected routes.

D: Execute sudo iptables -L to list all the active rules applied to the firewall.

Correct Answer: D

Explanation: Displaying firewall rules is crucial to understanding any changes that might have inadvertently opened up the network to external threats. The iptables -L command provides a clear list of all rules that apply to the firewall, allowing for a straightforward review.

----

103. While reviewing system logs, a technician discovers entries that are inconsistent with known patterns. What type of software might be used to automate the identification of such anomalies?

A: Implement an intrusion detection system (IDS) software like Snort to monitor network traffic and detect unusual patterns.

B: Engage a threat intelligence platform to gather and analyze information about potential security threats.

C: Install antivirus software to scan for and remove malware based on known signatures.

D: Utilize a system integrity checker like Tripwire to compare current system state to known good baselines.

Correct Answer: A

Explanation: An IDS like Snort specializes in analyzing network traffic to detect intrusions and suspicious activities by comparing against a database of known attack signatures and patterns, making it ideal for identifying inconsistencies in system logs.

----

104. During a security breach, it is found that unauthorized access was gained through an SSH server. To improve security, which configuration should be modified in the SSH server's settings?

A: Change the default SSH port from 22 to a non-standard port to reduce the risk of automated attacks.

B: Enforce a strict password policy requiring complex passwords that must be changed regularly.

C: Implement two-factor authentication for SSH access to enhance security credentials.

D: Enable full disk encryption on the server to secure data at rest and prevent unauthorized access.

Correct Answer: A

Explanation: Changing the default SSH port from 22 to a less commonly used port is a simple yet effective method to deter automated attacks and scans targeting default SSH ports, reducing the server's visibility to potential attackers.

----

105. Given a scenario where an attacker is using a compromised email account to send phishing emails within a company, which step should a cybersecurity technician take first to mitigate the attack?

A: Reset all user passwords company-wide to prevent further unauthorized access.

B: Isolate the compromised email server from the network to prevent the spread of phishing emails.

C: Increase email security by updating SPF, DKIM, and DMARC records to prevent email spoofing.

D: Conduct a forensic analysis of the email logs to identify the origin of the compromise and extent of the breach.

Correct Answer: D
Explanation: When an email account is compromised, analyzing email logs helps to quickly determine the source of the attack and the extent of the breach, enabling targeted remediation efforts and minimizing further damage.

----

106. To identify vulnerabilities on a network, a technician needs to scan all devices for outdated software and missing patches. Which tool should they use?

A: Implement Google dorks to find exposed credentials and sensitive directories through search engines.

B: Install NetStumbler to monitor network traffic and identify unauthorized access points.

C: Deploy SolarWinds Network Performance Monitor to track network performance and fault locations.

D: Use Nessus to conduct a comprehensive vulnerability scan that can detect outdated software and missing patches on networked devices.

Correct Answer: D
Explanation: Nessus is widely recognized for its effectiveness in scanning large networks to identify vulnerabilities like outdated software or missing patches, providing detailed reports that guide remediation efforts.

----

107. A security administrator needs to check for weak passwords in the organization. Which tool is most effective for this purpose?

A: Utilize Wireshark to analyze network traffic and identify weak encryption use.

B: Apply Hashcat to crack network hashes and expose password vulnerabilities.

C: Use Cain & Abel to decode saved passwords on a system and recover password boxes.

D: Employ John the Ripper to perform a password audit that identifies weak or easily guessable passwords.

Explanation: John the Ripper is a robust password testing tool that can detect weak passwords by performing comprehensive audits using various algorithms and dictionaries, thus helping secure accounts against brute-force attacks.

----

108. What command would a technician use to discover live hosts, open ports, and services on a network?

A: Use the command ping -a IP_range to resolve hostnames and verify active IP addresses.

B: Run traceroute -I target_IP to determine the path packets take to a host and identify network nodes.

C: Employ telnet target_IP to manually inspect the services running on a host machine.

D: Execute the command nmap -sV -O target_network to enumerate devices, services, and operating system details.

Explanation: The nmap -sV -O command is specifically designed to perform network scanning that includes service detection and operating system identification, which are crucial for effective network security management.

----

109. After detecting that a system might be vulnerable to script injections, what should a cybersecurity technician do first to mitigate this risk?

A: Restrict user privileges on the server to minimize the execution scope of any injected script.

B: Implement input validation checks to ensure all user inputs are sanitized before processing.

C: Upgrade all software to the latest versions to protect against known vulnerabilities.

D: Increase the security settings in the web server's configuration to automatically block scripts.

Correct Answer: B

Explanation: Input validation is a fundamental security measure for any application handling user input; it ensures that all data entered is strictly examined for malicious scripts, thus preventing script injection vulnerabilities.

----

110. In the context of web application security, what step should be taken to prevent SQL injection attacks on user input fields?

A: Institute regular security audits and vulnerability assessments to identify and mitigate risks periodically.

B: Enforce strict HTTPS protocols across all web applications to encrypt data transmissions.

C: Enable CAPTCHA on login pages to prevent automated scripts from executing login attempts.

D: Apply prepared statements with parameterized queries in database interactions to safeguard against SQL injection.

Correct Answer: D

Explanation: Using prepared statements with parameterized queries is a best practice in preventing SQL injection, one of the most common web application vulnerabilities, by separating SQL logic from data, thus ensuring that user input cannot alter the structure of SQL queries.

----

111. What is the most effective method to protect against phishing attacks targeting company executives?

A: Implement advanced email filtering solutions that can detect and block phishing attempts before they reach the user's inbox.

B: Conduct regular security awareness training for all employees to recognize phishing emails.

C: Increase the security settings on the company's email server to include manual checks of emails from unfamiliar sources.

D: Enforce a strict policy of verifying the sender's identity via phone before responding to email requests for sensitive information.

Correct Answer: A

Explanation: Advanced email filtering solutions are crucial in a corporate environment where executives are frequent targets of phishing. These systems use sophisticated algorithms to analyze incoming emails for signs of phishing, such as suspicious links or unexpected attachments, thereby blocking them before they reach the user.

----

112. To mitigate a DDoS attack, which network device should be configured to prevent excessive traffic reaching the company's servers?

A: Deploy an application delivery controller (ADC) that can provide load balancing and traffic management.

B: Install intrusion detection systems (IDS) to monitor network traffic for signs of a coordinated attack.

C: Use a content delivery network (CDN) to distribute the traffic load evenly across multiple servers.

D: Configure a network firewall with rate limiting rules to control incoming traffic and prevent overload.

Correct Answer: D
Explanation: Implementing rate limiting rules on a network firewall is an effective strategy to mitigate DDoS attacks. These rules help manage the flow of traffic, preventing the servers from becoming overwhelmed by excessive requests, which are typical in DDoS scenarios.

----

113. In response to detecting a network intrusion, which Linux command should be used to view currently established network connections?

A: Execute the command netstat -an | grep ESTABLISHED to filter out and display established connections.

B: Run lsof -i to display all network files, which indirectly shows active network connections.

C: Use the command ss -tuln to list active connections, their states, and listening ports to quickly identify unauthorized access.

D: Deploy iptables -L to review all firewall rules that could potentially block or allow specific traffic.

Correct Answer: C
Explanation: The command ss -tuln provides a detailed overview of network connections, including those that are established, making it a valuable tool for identifying suspicious or unauthorized connections that could indicate an intrusion.

----

114. When setting up a website, which configuration should be implemented to prevent cross-site scripting (XSS) attacks?

A: Apply a secure socket layer (SSL) certificate to encrypt data transmitted between the user and the website.

B: Implement HTTP Strict Transport Security (HSTS) to force HTTPS connections, enhancing secure communication.

C: Set cookies to HTTPOnly to prevent client-side scripts from accessing data stored in cookies.

D: Enable Content Security Policy (CSP) headers to restrict resources the browser is allowed to load, mitigating potential XSS exploits.

Correct Answer: D
Explanation: Content Security Policy (CSP) headers are an essential security measure for web applications, as they help mitigate XSS attacks by restricting how resources such as scripts, images, or stylesheets are loaded on the web page, effectively preventing malicious data execution.

----

115. Fill in the blank: To analyze network traffic and detect potential security breaches, use the _____ tool.

A: Wireshark

B: Tcpdump

C: Netcat

D: Nmap

Correct Answer: A
Explanation: Wireshark is a network protocol analyzer that allows users to capture and interactively browse the traffic running on a computer network. It is used extensively for network troubleshooting, analysis, software and protocol development, and education, making it an indispensable tool for security analysts monitoring for anomalies.

----

116. Which configuration ensures secure management of networking devices via remote access?

A: Use Telnet for remote device configuration to ensure all commands are logged.

B: Configure devices to only accept SSH (Secure Shell) for remote management connections.

C: Set up RDP (Remote Desktop Protocol) with standard authentication for device management.

D: Enable SNMP (Simple Network Management Protocol) version 2 for network device administration.

Correct Answer: B

Explanation: SSH is essential for secure remote management as it provides strong authentication and encrypted data communications, reducing the risk of eavesdropping and connection hijacking, which are common in unsecured protocols like Telnet.

----

117. What protocol should be implemented to securely encapsulate IP packets for transmission over a public network?

A: Implement IPsec (Internet Protocol Security) to encrypt and authenticate IP packets.

B: Adopt SSL (Secure Sockets Layer) for securing messages in the network layer.

C: Apply GRE (Generic Routing Encapsulation) to encapsulate a wide variety of network layer protocols.

D: Utilize the L2TP (Layer 2 Tunneling Protocol) alone to provide data confidentiality via tunneling.

Correct Answer: A

Explanation: IPsec is specifically designed for securing IP communications by encrypting and authenticating all IP packet transfers, making it ideal for protecting data that traverses across insecure networks such as the internet.

----

118. In securing a corporate network, which device is best placed between a company's internal network and the internet?

A: Deploy an IDS (Intrusion Detection System) directly connected to the internet router.

B: Place a router with basic ACLs (Access Control Lists) at the network perimeter.

C: Use a proxy server to filter web traffic and provide caching services.

D: Install a network firewall to inspect and manage traffic entering and exiting the network.

Correct Answer: D

Explanation: A network firewall acts as a barrier between a trusted internal network and untrusted external networks, such as the internet, by controlling traffic based on security rules, thereby preventing unauthorized access.

----

119. Fill in the blank: To monitor and control incoming and outgoing network traffic based on predetermined security rules, configure a _____.

A: Switch

B: Proxy

C: Firewall

D: Router

Correct Answer: C

Explanation: A firewall is a network security system that monitors and controls incoming and outgoing network traffic based on predetermined security rules. This setup is critical in defining the boundaries of security within the network infrastructure.

----

120. During a security assessment, it is discovered that internal traffic between departments is not isolated. What network design should be implemented to enhance security?

A: Introduce a unified threat management (UTM) device to handle all security processes.

B: Segment the network into VLANs (Virtual Local Area Networks) to control traffic flow and increase security.

C: Implement an MPLS (Multiprotocol Label Switching) architecture to speed up traffic flow and reduce latency.

D: Utilize a hub to connect segments of the internal network and monitor traffic.

Correct Answer: B

Explanation: VLANs are used to segment network traffic logically, which effectively isolates traffic in a network environment. This isolation helps reduce chances of security breaches as it controls which resources each network segment can access, enhancing overall network security.

----

121. A security administrator needs to enforce multi-factor authentication (MFA) on the company's systems. Which method should they use to verify the user's identity in addition to a password?

A: Set up an authenticator app on the user's smartphone, generating a time-based one-time password (TOTP) for the second authentication factor.

B: Implement SMS-based verification, sending a one-time code to the user's mobile phone for identity confirmation.

C: Install a biometric fingerprint scanner that requires users to scan their fingerprints in addition to entering a password.

D: Send a one-time link to the user's registered email address for second-factor verification.

Correct Answer: A
Explanation: A time-based one-time password (TOTP) generated through an authenticator app adds a strong layer of security beyond a password, ensuring that even if a password is compromised, the account remains protected by requiring the second factor.

\-

122. What command should be executed on a Linux system to create a new user and define an initial password for secure authentication?

A: Run useradd -m username -p password to create a user account with a pre-defined password and home directory.

B: Use adduser username && passwd username to create the user account and specify the password securely.

C: Apply usermod -aG username to create the user with default settings and assign privileges.

D: Execute sudo useradd username && sudo passwd username to create a new user and set the user's password.

Correct Answer: D
Explanation: The sudo useradd username && sudo passwd username command creates a new user securely on a Linux system and prompts for an initial password, establishing a basic authentication method for system access.

\-

123. To control user access to specific network resources based on their job roles, which technology should a network administrator implement?

A: Implement role-based access control (RBAC) to assign user permissions based on roles within the organization.

B: Deploy mandatory access control (MAC) policies to control access based on security labels and clearances.

C: Apply attribute-based access control (ABAC) to allow access based on attributes like location, time, and device type.

D: Utilize identity-based access control (IBAC) to manage permissions based on individual user identity.

Explanation: Role-based access control (RBAC) is the most efficient way to manage user permissions according to their job function, ensuring that each user has only the necessary access to perform their duties, thus minimizing the risk of privilege abuse.

----

124. Fill in the blank: To ensure secure access to web applications, configure _____ to manage user authentication via digital certificates.

A: Set up a Kerberos authentication server to manage secure access to network resources.

B: Integrate LDAP (Lightweight Directory Access Protocol) for centralized authentication and access control across the network.

C: Configure a Public Key Infrastructure (PKI) system to handle certificate-based user authentication and access control.

D: Use OAuth 2.0 to authenticate users through social media credentials or third-party services.

Correct Answer: C

Explanation: Public Key Infrastructure (PKI) allows for robust authentication using digital certificates, ensuring that only users with valid certificates can access web applications securely, protecting against identity spoofing.

----

125. During an audit, it was found that multiple users have unnecessary administrative privileges. Which access control model should be applied to restrict users' access based on their job responsibilities?

A: Set up a zero-trust model where users need to be continuously verified through their activity and device.

B: Establish a hybrid approach using both role-based and attribute-based access control for flexible privilege management.

C: Apply the principle of least privilege through RBAC to assign only necessary permissions to each user based on their job role.

D: Enforce access control policies through a discretionary access control (DAC) model to allow users to set permissions on their resources.

Correct Answer: C

Explanation: The principle of least privilege enforced through RBAC limits user access strictly to the resources required by their job role, minimizing the chances of accidental or malicious misuse of administrative privileges.

----

126. A cybersecurity manager is tasked with creating a policy for employees regarding acceptable use of the company's network. Which administrative control should be included to ensure compliance with this policy?

A: Create a physical access control system that tracks who enters and leaves the building to ensure compliance with network policies.

B: Deploy monitoring tools that automatically log network activity to identify any policy violations.

C: Enforce encryption of all company communications and documents to prevent accidental data leaks and ensure compliance.

D: Develop an Acceptable Use Policy (AUP) outlining permitted and prohibited activities on the company's network and require all employees to sign it.

Correct Answer: D

Explanation: An Acceptable Use Policy (AUP) clearly defines the acceptable activities that employees can engage in on the company's network. Requiring employees to sign the policy ensures that they are aware of the rules and the potential consequences for violations.

----

127. To comply with international security standards, an organization needs to implement a framework that guides their risk management process. Which framework should they adopt to align their policies with industry best practices?

A: Establish an ITIL framework to manage IT services and ensure continuous service improvement within the organization.

B: Adopt the COBIT framework to standardize and control IT management and governance practices within the organization.

C: Implement the ISO 27001 framework to create an Information Security Management System (ISMS) that addresses risk management.

D: Use the NIST Cybersecurity Framework to manage and reduce cybersecurity risk across the organization's networks.

Correct Answer: C

Explanation: ISO 27001 provides a comprehensive framework for creating and maintaining an Information Security Management System (ISMS). It is widely recognized for its focus on managing security risks through structured policies and procedures, ensuring alignment with international standards.

----

128. During an internal audit, it was discovered that there is no formal process for handling security incidents. What administrative control should be put in place to ensure a coordinated response to future incidents?

A: Implement a disaster recovery plan to ensure the organization can continue to operate in the event of an incident.

B: Outsource incident response to a third-party service to handle security incidents more efficiently.

C: Use continuous monitoring techniques to detect and respond to incidents without requiring a formal response plan.

D: Establish a formal Incident Response Plan (IRP) that outlines roles, responsibilities, and procedures for managing security incidents.

Correct Answer: D

Explanation: A formal Incident Response Plan (IRP) is critical in defining the roles, responsibilities, and processes for managing security incidents. It ensures that all staff know what to do in the event of a breach, minimizing the impact of security incidents.

----

129. Fill in the blank: To ensure compliance with data protection laws, organizations should establish a _____ policy that defines how personal data is collected, processed, and stored.

A: Data Privacy

B: Network Monitoring

C: Records Management

D: Email Filtering

Correct Answer: A

Explanation: A Data Privacy policy is essential for compliance with data protection laws, outlining how personal data is collected, processed, and stored. This helps protect organizations from legal and regulatory violations while securing customer and employee data.

----

130. A company wants to mitigate insider threats and ensure that sensitive information is only accessible to authorized personnel. Which administrative control should be implemented to enforce this?

A: Enforce a mandatory Security Awareness Training program, educating employees on the importance of safeguarding sensitive information.

B: Enforce two-factor authentication (2FA) to prevent unauthorized access to sensitive information.

C: Restrict employee access to the company's internal network during non-business hours to prevent insider threats.

D: Implement role-based access control (RBAC) to limit access to sensitive systems based on job functions.

Correct Answer: A

Explanation: Security Awareness Training ensures that employees are informed about the importance of protecting sensitive information. This control mitigates insider threats by educating employees on how to recognize and respond to security risks, reducing the likelihood of accidental or malicious data exposure.

----

131. To secure the server room in a company, which physical security measure should be implemented to control access?

A: Set up physical barriers such as gates and fences around the server room to limit access points.

B: Implement electronic door locks that use a card swipe system to control access to the server room.

C: Use biometric access control systems to restrict entry to authorized personnel only.

D: Install a keypad access system that requires users to enter a unique code to gain entry to the server room.

Correct Answer: C

Explanation: Biometric access control systems are highly secure because they rely on unique biological traits like fingerprints or retina scans, ensuring that only authorized personnel can access critical areas like the server room, thereby significantly reducing the risk of unauthorized access.

----

132. What is the best method to ensure physical protection of network equipment located in an open office environment?

A: Install lockable server racks to secure equipment, preventing unauthorized physical access.

B: Install floor-to-ceiling partitions to enclose network devices and prevent unauthorized access.

C: Use motion-detecting alarms to alert security personnel to unauthorized access.

D: Place security personnel near critical equipment to monitor for suspicious activity and prevent unauthorized access.

Correct Answer: A
Explanation: Lockable server racks provide physical security for network devices in open office environments, preventing unauthorized individuals from tampering with or stealing equipment by restricting direct access to the hardware.

----

133. During a site assessment, it was found that the data center has no monitoring systems. What physical control should be implemented to enhance security?

A: Apply a mantrap at the entrance to the data center to prevent tailgating and ensure secure access.

B: Install proximity sensors that activate alarms when movement is detected in secure areas during off-hours.

C: Install fire suppression systems and temperature monitoring to protect equipment from environmental hazards.

D: Implement CCTV surveillance cameras that monitor activity in the data center 24/7.

Correct Answer: D
Explanation: CCTV surveillance cameras provide continuous monitoring of the data center, recording all activity and offering real-time visual evidence of any unauthorized or suspicious behavior. This increases overall security by deterring potential intruders.

----

134. Fill in the blank: To prevent unauthorized access to network devices, install _____ to log and track all entry and exit events at secure locations.

A: Metal detectors

B: Smart locks

C: Badge readers

D: Security gates

Correct Answer: C

Explanation: Badge readers help ensure that only authorized individuals can enter secure areas by logging entry and exit data. This creates an audit trail, allowing administrators to track who accessed specific locations and when.

----

135. A company noticed several incidents of hardware theft over the past year. What physical security measure should be implemented to secure high-value equipment?

A: Deploy asset tagging with RFID tracking to monitor the location of valuable hardware.

B: Lock devices to desks using cable locks to prevent theft of small portable devices.

C: Increase security patrol frequency in high-risk areas and enforce stricter visitor sign-in procedures.

D: Use tamper-evident security seals on high-value equipment to detect unauthorized access or removal.

Correct Answer: A

Explanation: Asset tagging with RFID tracking allows organizations to monitor the physical location of valuable hardware in real time, reducing the risk of theft by enabling quick detection of unauthorized movement or removal of high-value equipment.

----

136. When configuring a SIEM system to ensure accurate and comprehensive logging of security events, what should be the primary consideration in the setup process to enhance network security and data correlation capabilities?

A: Choosing a SIEM that offers real-time event correlation to handle high volumes of data.

B: Selecting a centralized management platform for all security tools to streamline incident response.

C: Ensuring that log sources are properly configured to report all relevant security events without filtering or aggregation.

D: Integrating SIEM with network infrastructure for automated remediation actions against detected threats.

Explanation: Configuring log sources to capture all security events is crucial for a SIEM system as it relies heavily on log data to perform event correlation and analysis. Without comprehensive and accurate data, the effectiveness of a SIEM system in detecting and responding to threats is significantly diminished.

----

137. Given a network infrastructure that includes an IDS and a firewall, what command should an administrator use to verify that the IDS is correctly capturing traffic without dropping packets due to misconfiguration?

A: ping 192.168.1.1 -c 4

B: nmap -sP 192.168.1.0/24

C: tcpdump -i eth0 not port 22

D: iftop

Correct Answer: C
Explanation: Using tcpdump -i eth0 not port 22 allows the administrator to monitor network traffic on interface eth0 while excluding SSH traffic (port 22), providing a clear view of all other traffic for analysis without the common clutter of encrypted SSH data. This ensures that the IDS is capturing the necessary traffic for security monitoring.

----

138. Fill in the blank: To optimize the performance of a network-based IDS, the _____ should be adjusted to balance between security monitoring effectiveness and system resource usage.

A: capture filters

B: threshold limits

C: buffer sizes

D: signature database versions

Correct Answer: B
Explanation: Adjusting threshold limits in a network-based IDS is essential to manage the volume of alerts generated. This balance prevents the system from being overwhelmed by false positives while ensuring genuine threats are not missed, optimizing both security effectiveness and resource usage.

----

139. In a scenario where a security team is tasked with implementing a new firewall rule to block all incoming traffic from a specific IP address, which command is most appropriate for creating this rule on a Linux-based firewall system?

A: route add -net 192.168.1.0 netmask 255.255.255.0 gw 192.168.1.1

B: nc -l 8080

C: iptables -A INPUT -s 192.168.1.1 -j DROP

D: netstat -an | grep LISTEN

Correct Answer: C

Explanation: The command iptables -A INPUT -s 192.168.1.1 -j DROP effectively blocks all incoming traffic from the specified IP address. It appends a rule to the input chain to drop packets from this source, enhancing the security posture by preventing potentially harmful traffic from entering the network.

----

140. A company's network security team is planning to deploy a SIEM solution. They must decide which data sources are most critical for early threat detection. Which of the following would be the least effective source to prioritize for early threat detection?

A: Anti-virus scan reports

B: Network performance metrics

C: Firewall log files

D: Application error logs

Correct Answer: B

Explanation: Network performance metrics, while useful for maintaining the health of network infrastructure, do not directly contribute to threat detection in a SIEM context. Prioritizing logs from sources directly involved in security, such as firewalls or application logs, would be more beneficial for early detection of security incidents.

----

141. A network technician suspects there is an issue with packet loss on the corporate network. What command should be used to identify and monitor the packet loss rate between your host and a remote server?

A: ipconfig /all

B: netstat -r

C: mtr google.com

D: ping -t google.com

Correct Answer: D
Explanation: The ping -t google.com command continuously sends ICMP echo requests to the target, allowing the technician to observe the packet loss rate over time. This method provides real-time feedback on the stability and reliability of the network path to the server, which is essential for diagnosing intermittent network problems.

----

142. In diagnosing network connectivity issues, which tool should be used to trace the path packets take from a computer to a host across an IP network?
A: traceroute www.example.com

B: nslookup www.example.com

C: ping www.example.com

D: arp -a

Correct Answer: A
Explanation: The traceroute www.example.com tool is used to display the path that packets take to reach a host. It lists all intermediate routers through which the packets pass, allowing the technician to identify at which hop the packets are being dropped or delayed, crucial for pinpointing routing issues in the network.

----

143. Fill in the blank: To check the operational status and speed of the network interfaces on a Linux system, the command _____ should be executed.
A: nmcli device status

B: ifconfig -a

C: ethtool eth0

D: iwconfig

Correct Answer: C
Explanation: The ethtool eth0 command is utilized to display and modify settings of an Ethernet device. It provides detailed information about the link status, speed, and other network parameters, making it invaluable for verifying the physical layer and Ethernet link operation, which are often the first areas to troubleshoot in network issues.

----

144. You need to troubleshoot a sudden issue with DNS resolution failure in your network. Which command will provide detailed query information that can help diagnose the problem?

A: host -a www.example.com

B: nslookup -debug www.example.com

C: whois www.example.com

D: dig +trace www.example.com

Correct Answer: D

Explanation: Utilizing dig +trace www.example.com enables the user to see the path that a DNS query takes to resolve a domain name to an IP address. This command provides a step-by-step trace of the DNS resolution process, showing all DNS servers involved and helping to identify where the resolution may be failing.

----

145. During a network outage, a technician needs to verify if the router gateway is reachable and functioning. Which command would be most effective in confirming this without generating excessive network traffic?

A: ping -c 1 gateway_ip_address

B: arping gateway_ip_address

C: traceroute gateway_ip_address

D: netstat -rn

Correct Answer: A

Explanation: The ping -c 1 gateway_ip_address command sends a single ICMP echo request to the network's gateway to check for basic connectivity. This approach minimizes the network traffic caused by the test, which is particularly useful during an outage or when network stability is a concern.

----

146. To effectively monitor network traffic anomalies, which command allows real-time traffic analysis and content-based logging?

A: netstat -s

B: tcpdump -A -i eth0

C: wireshark -k -i eth0

D: nmap -T4 -A -v

Correct Answer: B

Explanation: The command tcpdump -A -i eth0 is essential for monitoring network traffic as it captures each packet that flows through the interface eth0 and prints each packet in ASCII format, making it easier to spot anomalies in the content of the packets. This is particularly useful for identifying unusual patterns or potential security threats in real-time.

----

147. Which configuration should be implemented on an IDS to increase its effectiveness in capturing and analyzing encrypted traffic?

A: Enable Deep Packet Inspection (DPI)

B: Implement stateful packet inspection

C: Configure packet mirroring

D: Use traffic flow analysis

Correct Answer: A

Explanation: Enabling Deep Packet Inspection (DPI) on an IDS is crucial for analyzing encrypted traffic. DPI examines the data part (and possibly also the header) of the packets as they pass an inspection point, enabling the IDS to detect potential malicious packets that could be hidden in encrypted traffic. This enhances the security measures by providing a deeper inspection beyond just header data.

----

148. Fill in the blank: For detailed network traffic analysis, the _____ utility is preferred for capturing and displaying header information and packet payloads.

A: nmap

B: wireshark

C: tcpdump

D: netstat

Correct Answer: C

Explanation: tcpdump is a powerful command-line packet analyzer; it allows the capture or filter TCP/IP packets that are received or transferred over a network. It provides a detailed view of the headers and payloads of the packets, facilitating an extensive examination of incoming and outgoing traffic to diagnose potential issues or anomalies.

----

149. A network security analyst needs to configure a tool to alert when unusual traffic patterns, such as unexpected access from foreign IP addresses, are detected. Which tool is best suited for this job?

A: Set up anomaly-based intrusion detection

B: Apply geo-IP filtering at the router level

C: Enhance the firewall with additional filtering rules

D: Configure signature-based detection settings

Correct Answer: A

Explanation: Setting up anomaly-based intrusion detection systems is critical for identifying unexpected patterns that deviate from established norms, such as connections from foreign IP addresses. These systems use algorithms to detect unusual patterns that may indicate malicious activity, providing alerts for further investigation.

----

150. During an investigation of network slowdown, which command should a technician use to display traffic summaries grouped by protocol type and ensure all traffic types are accounted for?

A: etherape

B: iftop

C: iptraf -d eth0

D: ntop -P

Correct Answer: D

Explanation: The ntop -P command is highly effective for monitoring network traffic, as it provides a visual representation of network traffic by protocol type, helping technicians to quickly identify if any specific protocol is unusually dominant, which could be a sign of a network issue or a security breach. This tool aggregates traffic into graphs that can be easily interpreted to monitor network health and performance.

----

151. What command should be used to monitor live system log updates on a Linux server for real-time intrusion detection?

A: cat /var/log/syslog

B: tail -f /var/log/syslog

C: less /var/log/syslog

D: watch "cat /var/log/syslog"

Correct Answer: B

Explanation: The tail -f /var/log/syslog command is essential for monitoring live updates of system logs. It allows security administrators to view the most recent parts of a log file in real-time, making it easier to spot unauthorized access or suspicious activities as they occur.

----

152. When configuring a SIEM for optimal performance, what is the most critical factor to consider to ensure effective log analysis and threat detection?

A: User access permissions for log files

B: Storage capacity for historical log data

C: The geographical location of log storage

D: Real-time log processing and event correlation

Correct Answer: D

Explanation: Real-time log processing and event correlation are crucial for a SIEM system as they enable the immediate analysis of log data to detect patterns and anomalies that may indicate security threats. This capability ensures timely responses to potential security incidents, enhancing the overall effectiveness of log monitoring systems.

----

153. Fill in the blank: To analyze Windows security logs for signs of intrusion, the _____ PowerShell cmdlet is extremely useful for filtering event logs based on specific criteria.

A: Set-EventLog

B: Read-EventLog

C: Get-EventLog

D: Update-EventLog

Correct Answer: C

Explanation: The Get-EventLog PowerShell cmdlet is designed to retrieve event logs, which can be filtered by various parameters such as the event ID, log name, and machine name. This makes it an indispensable tool for Windows administrators looking to sift through security logs to find specific entries related to intrusion attempts.

----

154. A security analyst suspects an unauthorized access attempt on a network. Which command will help analyze login attempts from the system logs to confirm this suspicion?

A: tail -n 100 /var/log/auth.log

B: cat /var/log/auth.log | less

C: awk '/Failed password/ {print}' /var/log/auth.log

D: grep "Failed password" /var/log/auth.log

Correct Answer: D

Explanation: Using grep "Failed password" /var/log/auth.log helps in identifying failed login attempts by filtering the authentication log for specific entries related to password failures. This is a straightforward method to detect unauthorized access attempts, providing clear evidence if an account has been targeted.

----

155. In setting up a log monitoring solution, what configuration must be implemented to automatically alert administrators when critical errors or security breaches are detected in server logs?

A: Configure alerts for log events with severity "critical" or higher

B: Enable log rotation for files larger than 10 MB

C: Set up weekly log audits and reviews

D: Implement a redundant logging database

Correct Answer: A

Explanation: Configuring alerts for log events with severity "critical" or higher is a fundamental security practice. This setup ensures that administrators receive immediate notifications about serious issues, enabling quick action to mitigate threats and resolve critical errors promptly, thereby maintaining the integrity and security of the IT environment.

----

156. Which command is used to display the encryption status of Wi-Fi networks detected by a Linux-based machine?

A: nmap -sP 192.168.1.0/24

B: iwconfig wlan0

C: netsh wlan show networks mode=bssid

D: iwlist wlan0 scanning | grep Encryption

Correct Answer: D
Explanation: The command iwlist wlan0 scanning | grep Encryption is effective for identifying the encryption status of all visible wireless networks. This command provides specific details on whether each network is secured and by what method of encryption, which is crucial for assessing the security level of Wi-Fi networks within range.

----

157. When setting up a new wireless network, which encryption standard is considered the most secure to protect against unauthorized access?

A: WPA

B: WPA3

C: WEP

D: WPA2

Correct Answer: B
Explanation: WPA3 is the latest and most secure wireless encryption standard, providing stronger protections against offline dictionary attacks compared to its predecessors, WPA and WPA2. Its adoption ensures the highest level of security for network communications.

----

158. Fill in the blank: For advanced configuration of wireless security on a router, accessing the web interface typically requires entering the IP address, such as _____ into a web browser.

A: 10.0.0.1

B: 192.168.1.1

C: 192.168.100.1

D: 192.168.0.1

Correct Answer: B

Explanation: The IP address 192.168.1.1 is commonly used to access the router's web interface for configuration purposes. It is a standard gateway address used by many routers, making it the first address that should be tried when attempting to configure wireless settings via a browser.

\-

159. A network administrator wants to verify the security protocol used by all connected devices to a corporate Wi-Fi network. Which tool should be used to perform this check?

A: Wireshark

B: Kismet

C: AirSnort

D: NetStumbler

Correct Answer: A

Explanation: Wireshark is a network protocol analyzer that can capture and display the packets traveling over a network. It is particularly useful for verifying the encryption protocols used by devices connected to a Wi-Fi network, as it can analyze the handshake process and the security mechanisms in place.

\-

160. During a security audit, a technician needs to evaluate the strength of the WPA2 passphrase used in the company's wireless network. Which technique is appropriate for this purpose?

A: Password cracking with a dictionary attack

B: Manually checking the passphrase complexity

C: Observing network traffic with packet sniffing

D: Implementing a honeypot network to attract attacks

Correct Answer: A

Explanation: Using a password cracking tool that employs a dictionary attack can help assess the strength of a WPA2 passphrase by attempting to match it against a list of commonly used passwords and phrases. This technique highlights potential vulnerabilities in passphrase strength and encourages the use of more complex passwords to enhance security.

\-

161. What is the recommended command to check for security patches on an Android device using the ADB tool?

A: adb update -a

B: adb install -k

C: adb shell getprop ro.build.version.security_patch

D: adb reboot bootloader

Correct Answer: C
Explanation: The command adb shell getprop ro.build.version.security_patch provides the date of the last security patch applied to an Android device. Knowing the patch level is essential for understanding the device's vulnerability status and ensuring it is up-to-date with the latest security measures to prevent exploitation.

----

162. To enhance security on iOS devices, which setting should be enabled to ensure that data is encrypted when the device is locked?

A: Enable 'Find My iPhone'

B: Auto-lock screen after 2 minutes

C: Turn on 'Limit Ad Tracking'

D: Data Protection by enabling passcode

Correct Answer: D
Explanation: Enabling Data Protection by setting a passcode on iOS devices encrypts the data stored on the device when it is locked. This encryption makes it difficult for unauthorized users to access sensitive information if the device is lost or stolen, significantly enhancing data security.

----

163. Fill in the blank: To improve security against malware, mobile devices should have _____ installed that can detect and respond to malicious activities.

A: encrypted storage

B: antivirus software

C: VPN service

D: firewall application

Correct Answer: B

Explanation: Installing antivirus software on mobile devices is critical for detecting and mitigating malware infections. Such software continuously monitors the device for signs of malicious activity, providing necessary protection against a variety of threats that could compromise data and functionality.

----

164. A company's IT department wants to ensure that all employees' mobile devices are configured with the correct security settings. What is the best approach to manage these settings across multiple devices efficiently?

A: Use group policy over a corporate network

B: Distribute a standard configuration guide to employees

C: Manual configuration by IT staff member by member

D: Implement Mobile Device Management (MDM) software

Correct Answer: D

Explanation: Implementing Mobile Device Management (MDM) software allows IT departments to configure and enforce security policies across all mobile devices in the organization centrally. This approach ensures consistent security settings, including password policies and encryption, across all devices, reducing the risk of data breaches.

----

165. During a routine security check, you need to verify if any mobile applications on a device have unnecessary permissions that could risk data exposure. Which approach is most effective?

A: Disable unused apps through device settings

B: Regularly reset device to factory settings

C: Use a mobile security app to audit application permissions

D: Review app permissions manually in device settings

Correct Answer: C

Explanation: Using a mobile security app to audit application permissions on a device helps identify and manage app permissions effectively. Such apps provide detailed insights into which apps have access to sensitive data and functions, allowing users to revoke unnecessary permissions that could be exploited by malicious actors.

----

166. What command should be used on a network router to segregate IoT devices into a separate VLAN for security purposes?

A: set vlan IoT devices

B: config vlan 200 name IoT-VLAN

C: create vlan-id 400 name IoT

D: add IoT-network vlan 300

Correct Answer: B

Explanation: Creating a VLAN specifically for IoT devices helps isolate network traffic, which can reduce the risk of cross-device interference and enhance security by confining potential breaches to a controlled environment.

----

167. In an IoT environment, which configuration ensures that device firmware updates are securely transmitted and applied?

A: Installing anti-virus software on each IoT device

B: Disabling unused services and protocols on devices

C: Mandatory multifactor authentication for device access

D: Enabling encrypted communication channels and automated patch management

Correct Answer: D

Explanation: Encrypted communications prevent eavesdropping and tampering with the firmware updates during transmission, while automated patch management ensures that devices are always updated with the latest security patches without manual intervention, minimizing vulnerability exposure.

----

168. Fill in the blank: To improve IoT security, devices should be configured to communicate only with _____ servers.

A: trusted

B: external

C: unauthorized

D: local

Correct Answer: A

Explanation: Restricting IoT devices to communicate only with trusted servers prevents data leakage and unauthorized access by ensuring that all data flows between the devices and approved endpoints, which are verified and secured.

----

169. A smart home security system IoT device needs a secure protocol for sending video feeds over the internet. Which protocol should be used?

A: Hyper Text Transfer Protocol Secure (HTTPS)

B: Multipurpose Internet Mail Extensions (MIME) over SSL

C: Secure File Transfer Protocol (SFTP)

D: Real-Time Streaming Protocol (RTSP) over TLS

Correct Answer: D

Explanation: RTSP over TLS provides a secure channel for streaming media by encrypting the video feed, which protects against interception and ensures that data privacy and integrity are maintained while streaming over potentially unsecured networks.

----

170. Given the scenario of a distributed network of IoT devices monitoring environmental data, which security measure would prevent a single compromised device from jeopardizing the entire network's integrity?

A: Applying uniform security policies across all devices without exceptions

B: Regularly updating all devices with the same security patches simultaneously

C: Implementing network segmentation and individual device authentication

D: Ensuring all devices are connected to the internet for constant monitoring

Correct Answer: C

Explanation: Network segmentation allows each IoT device or group of devices to operate independently within separate network segments. This approach limits the spread of potential attacks across the network, and individual device authentication ensures that each device's identity is verified before it can connect to the network, further enhancing security measures.

----

171. When configuring an industrial firewall to secure a network with PLCs controlling assembly lines, which rule best secures traffic?

A: Allowing all outgoing traffic unless specifically flagged by threat intelligence tools

B: Restricting all external remote access unless it passes through a VPN with strong encryption

C: Blocking all incoming traffic that does not originate from known internal IP addresses

D: Permitting traffic only during certain hours when monitoring is actively conducted by security personnel

Correct Answer: C
Explanation: Blocking all non-originating internal IP traffic ensures that unauthorized external access is prevented, thus safeguarding sensitive PLC operations from potential cyber threats that could disrupt the assembly line operations.

----

172. Which strategy should be implemented first when designing a security policy for an OT network containing legacy systems?

A: Immediately updating all systems to the latest software versions without a prior risk analysis

B: Requiring dual-factor authentication for all users accessing OT systems, regardless of their role

C: Conducting a comprehensive vulnerability assessment to identify and prioritize risks

D: Creating isolated networks for different parts of the OT infrastructure without assessing interaction needs

Correct Answer: C
Explanation: A comprehensive vulnerability assessment allows for an understanding of existing weaknesses, especially in legacy systems, and helps prioritize the implementation of security measures based on the severity of identified risks.

----

173. Fill in the blank: In an OT network, it is essential to _____ before performing any system updates to avoid operational disruption.

A: install updates

B: log activity

C: validate connectivity

D: create backups

Correct Answer: D
Explanation: Creating backups is a fundamental security practice in OT environments, ensuring that operations can be restored quickly with minimal downtime in the event of a system update failure or after a cyber-attack.

----

174. During a security audit of an OT system, which action should be prioritized to protect against external threats?
A: Increasing password complexity requirements across all devices and systems in the OT network

B: Applying regular patches to all OT devices regardless of their criticality or function within the network

C: Implementing strict lockout policies after several failed access attempts to prevent brute force attacks

D: Segmenting the network to restrict access between the corporate IT environment and the OT systems

Correct Answer: D
Explanation: Network segmentation effectively isolates the OT systems from the broader IT environment, reducing the risk of cross-contamination from external threats and containing any potential breaches within controlled boundaries.

----

175. Given a scenario where an OT network is experiencing repeated security breaches, what is the most effective initial response?
A: Upgrading all outdated hardware to newer, more secure versions to close known vulnerabilities

B: Implementing real-time intrusion detection systems to monitor network traffic and alert anomalies

C: Replacing legacy systems with modern equivalents that have better security features and support

D: Conducting frequent password resets across all systems to prevent unauthorized access

Correct Answer: B
Explanation: Implementing a real-time intrusion detection system enables continuous monitoring of network activities, providing immediate alerts on unusual or potentially

harmful actions, thereby allowing for swift response before any significant damage can occur.

----

176. Which command would best configure a virtual machine (VM) to only accept traffic from the virtual switch within the same environment, enhancing its network security?

A: esxcli network firewall set --enabled true

B: iptables -A INPUT -s 192.168.0.0/24 -j ACCEPT

C: ovs-vsctl add-port br0 veth0

D: brctl addbr virtualswitch0

Correct Answer: A
Explanation: Configuring the VM to only accept traffic from the virtual switch within the environment using the firewall ensures that external traffic, including unauthorized traffic from outside the virtual network, is blocked, thus providing an additional layer of network security.

----

177. When securing a hypervisor in a virtualized environment, which approach should be used to minimize attack surface while ensuring operational stability?

A: Enabling all administrative tools to provide quick access for troubleshooting issues

B: Applying security patches on the hypervisor immediately upon release without prior testing

C: Setting up centralized logging for all hypervisor events without limiting log retention policies

D: Reducing unnecessary services and only enabling critical management functions

Correct Answer: D
Explanation: Reducing the services enabled on a hypervisor minimizes its attack surface, making it less susceptible to exploitation while maintaining critical functionality. This allows for better operational stability without exposing unnecessary services that could be exploited by attackers.

----

178. Fill in the blank: Before deploying a VM template to production, ensure that _____ is disabled to prevent attackers from using default credentials.

A: network bridging

B: guest access

C: shared permissions

D: admin services

Correct Answer: B
Explanation: Disabling guest access in VM templates is essential because default credentials are a common entry point for attackers. Ensuring guest access is disabled before deploying to production strengthens the overall security by removing this potential vulnerability.

----

179. A virtualized environment has multiple VMs running on the same host. If one VM is compromised, which strategy should be implemented to prevent lateral movement between the virtual machines?

A: Using default hypervisor settings to allow the hypervisor to manage VM traffic dynamically

B: Establishing a flat network structure within the virtualized environment for easier management

C: Isolating compromised VMs in a separate virtual LAN with limited access

D: Enabling strict inter-VM firewall rules within the hypervisor

Correct Answer: D
Explanation: Enabling strict inter-VM firewall rules ensures that traffic between VMs is tightly controlled, preventing lateral movement if one VM is compromised. This limits the ability of an attacker to compromise additional VMs, thereby containing the breach within one environment.

----

180. Given a scenario where a VM is exposed to the internet for hosting web services, which action would most effectively enhance the VM's security posture?

A: Implementing a host-based intrusion detection system with real-time alerting

B: Disabling unused virtual network adapters to reduce exposure to attacks

C: Limiting the number of virtual CPUs allocated to the VM to reduce processing capacity for attackers

D: Running a virtual firewall appliance that blocks all untrusted inbound connections

Explanation: Implementing a host-based intrusion detection system with real-time alerting allows for continuous monitoring of the VM, ensuring that any suspicious activity is immediately flagged. This proactive security measure enhances the VM's defense against external threats when exposed to the internet.

----

181. You are tasked with securing access to sensitive cloud storage using an identity-based access control policy. Which command best enforces the policy to restrict access to users with specific roles?

A: az role assignment create --assignee <user> --role "Storage Blob Data Contributor"

B: oci iam policy create --name "restricted_policy" --statements file://policy.json

C: gcloud projects add-iam-policy-binding my-project --member=user:example@gmail.com --role=roles/owner

D: aws iam create-policy --policy-name Access-Control --policy-document file://access-policy.json

Explanation: The command aws iam create-policy creates a custom policy that can define specific access controls for users, based on their roles. Using identity-based policies allows granular control over who can access sensitive resources, ensuring that only authorized users with the correct roles have permission.

----

182. What is the most secure configuration for protecting data at rest in cloud environments when deploying a new cloud database service?

A: Applying field-level encryption to only sensitive columns within the database using customer-managed keys

B: Leaving the encryption settings at default but applying strict access control lists (ACLs) for data access

C: Encrypting the entire database with customer-managed keys using cloud-native encryption tools

D: Encrypting the database at rest using provider-managed encryption keys with no additional configurations

Correct Answer: C
Explanation: Encrypting the database with customer-managed keys provides full control over the encryption process, offering stronger protection compared to provider-managed encryption. Customer-managed keys ensure that even the cloud provider cannot decrypt the data without the customer's permission.

----

183. Fill in the blank: To prevent unauthorized access to cloud resources, all remote access should be routed through a _____.

A: secure VPN

B: virtual network

C: dedicated subnet

D: application firewall

Correct Answer: A
Explanation: Routing all remote access through a secure VPN encrypts all traffic to the cloud environment, preventing unauthorized access. A VPN establishes a secure tunnel that ensures confidentiality and integrity for all communication, even over untrusted networks.

----

184. In a hybrid cloud deployment, a company's virtual machines need to communicate with on-premises resources securely. Which solution should be implemented to ensure secure communication?

A: Setting up encrypted communication using SSL/TLS certificates between the cloud and on-premises systems

B: Implementing an API gateway between the cloud and on-premises systems with TLS encryption

C: Enforcing IPsec tunneling for all traffic between cloud-based virtual machines and on-premises resources

D: Establishing a site-to-site VPN connection with encryption enabled between the cloud and on-premises environments

Correct Answer: D
Explanation: Establishing a site-to-site VPN connection between cloud and on-premises environments ensures that all data transmitted between the two environments is

encrypted. This provides secure communication for hybrid cloud deployments, preventing data from being exposed during transit.

---

185. Given a scenario where multiple users are uploading files to a shared cloud storage service, what is the best security measure to ensure that files are encrypted before they are uploaded?

A: Using client-side encryption to encrypt files locally before sending them to cloud storage

B: Using token-based encryption to encrypt files during the transfer to cloud storage services

C: Encrypting files at rest with the cloud provider's server-side encryption automatically upon upload

D: Automatically applying encryption policies in the cloud for all files uploaded via the user interface

Correct Answer: A

Explanation: Client-side encryption ensures that files are encrypted locally, before they are uploaded to the cloud, giving users full control over the encryption process. This guarantees that only encrypted data is stored in the cloud, and the cloud provider has no access to the encryption keys.

---

186. Which command would best configure a new VLAN on a switch to segment IoT devices from the main network for security purposes?

A: set vlan 30 name private-network

B: vlan 10 name IoT-devices

C: ip route add 192.168.10.0/24 dev vlan10

D: interface vlan 20 name secure-segment

Correct Answer: B

Explanation: Configuring a VLAN with a specific name, such as "IoT-devices," is the most effective way to isolate IoT devices from the rest of the network. VLANs logically separate network segments, allowing you to control which devices can communicate across the network.

---

187. In a corporate environment, a network administrator wants to isolate development servers from the production network. Which method would ensure that only specific traffic can pass between these segments?

A: Configuring Access Control Lists (ACLs) to control traffic between development and production networks

B: Applying network address translation (NAT) to block communication between development and production networks

C: Setting up a single flat network with firewall rules to block communication between development and production networks

D: Using port mirroring to monitor traffic between the development and production networks without blocking communication

Correct Answer: A

Explanation: Access Control Lists (ACLs) provide granular control over which traffic is allowed between different network segments, such as development and production environments. ACLs ensure that only authorized traffic can pass through, effectively securing these isolated segments.

----

188. Fill in the blank: When implementing network segmentation, _____ should be used to manage communication between different VLANs.

A: layer 3 routing

B: switch port trunk

C: network segmentation

D: DHCP relay

Correct Answer: A

Explanation: Layer 3 routing is necessary for managing communication between VLANs. Without routing between VLANs, devices on separate VLANs would not be able to communicate. Layer 3 devices like routers or layer 3 switches manage this process securely.

----

189. During a network audit, you discover that sensitive systems are accessible from the same network as guest Wi-Fi devices. What is the best approach to isolate these sensitive systems while maintaining guest Wi-Fi access?

A: Creating a single network for all devices but isolating sensitive systems through user permissions and access control

B: Using a flat network and deploying endpoint security solutions on the guest Wi-Fi devices

C: Establishing a shared network environment and encrypting sensitive traffic between systems

D: Creating separate VLANs for the guest Wi-Fi and sensitive systems, with firewall rules to block inter-VLAN traffic

Correct Answer: D

Explanation: By creating separate VLANs for the guest Wi-Fi and sensitive systems, you can apply firewall rules to block communication between them. This approach maintains access for guests while ensuring sensitive systems are isolated from potential threats.

----

190. A company is expanding and needs to ensure that its finance department's network is completely segmented from other departments. What should be implemented to restrict access between departments while allowing necessary internet access for all users?

A: Enforcing password policies across departments and applying encryption for sensitive data transmissions

B: Using IPsec tunneling to isolate sensitive communication between the finance department and other departments

C: Deploying a unified access control system across all networks with centralized authentication

D: Implementing private VLANs (PVLAN) to isolate the finance network from other departmental networks

Correct Answer: D

Explanation: Private VLANs (PVLANs) allow for isolation of specific departments, such as finance, from other departments while still providing necessary internet access. PVLANs restrict communication between departments, ensuring that only authorized traffic can pass, thereby protecting sensitive information.

----

191. Which command should be used to establish an IPsec VPN tunnel on a network device to provide secure remote access?

A: set vpn ipsec site-to-site peer 192.168.1.1 ike-group IKE-1

B: set vpn ipsec esp-group ESP-1 encryption aes128

C: set vpn l2tp remote-access authentication mode local

D: set ike-group IKE-1 proposal 1 dh-group 14

Correct Answer: A

Explanation: The command set vpn ipsec site-to-site peer establishes a secure IPsec tunnel between two network devices, ensuring that remote users can securely access internal resources by encrypting traffic between the sites. This provides end-to-end encryption and secures the connection.

----

192. To ensure secure communication over a public network, which configuration step is required when setting up a VPN to avoid IP address conflicts between the client and the internal network?

A: Implementing a double NAT (Network Address Translation) to ensure IP address translation between the client and internal network

B: Using split tunneling with separate IP ranges for internal and external traffic to prevent IP conflicts

C: Disabling IPsec rekeying intervals to prevent conflicts with dynamically assigned IP addresses

D: Using IP address pools assigned dynamically to avoid any conflicts during the VPN session

Correct Answer: B

Explanation: Split tunneling allows the VPN client to access internal resources without IP conflicts by routing only certain traffic through the VPN while using a separate range for internet traffic. This helps to prevent IP conflicts that could arise from overlapping addresses in the remote and internal networks.

----

193. Fill in the blank: A proxy server should be configured to route all traffic through a _____ to ensure encrypted communication between remote users and internal services.

A: secure enclave

B: secure VPN

C: trusted proxy

D: encrypted gateway

Correct Answer: B

Explanation: A secure VPN ensures that all traffic between the remote user and the internal network is encrypted. Configuring the proxy to route traffic through a secure VPN protects the data in transit and prevents exposure to external networks or potential threats.

----

194. A company wants to allow remote workers to securely access internal resources while ensuring that their internet traffic is routed through the corporate network. What is the best method to configure this?

A: Setting up a dual-homed proxy server to handle remote access while keeping internet traffic outside the VPN

B: Setting up split tunneling to allow internet traffic to bypass the VPN, but access internal resources through the VPN tunnel

C: Configuring full tunnel VPN access with all traffic routed through the corporate network

D: Deploying a DNS-based solution to resolve internal addresses while allowing public internet traffic to flow outside the VPN

Correct Answer: C

Explanation: Full tunnel VPN access routes all traffic, including internet traffic, through the corporate network, ensuring that the organization can monitor and secure all traffic. This configuration is crucial when the organization wants to ensure that all external traffic is filtered through its security policies.

----

195. A remote office needs to securely access an internal web server, but only HTTP traffic should be allowed through the VPN. How should the VPN configuration be adjusted to meet this requirement?

A: Enabling a specific firewall rule to allow only TCP port 80 traffic through the VPN tunnel

B: Configuring traffic shaping to give priority to HTTP traffic through the VPN tunnel

C: Enforcing specific proxy configurations to manage HTTP traffic through the VPN tunnel for added security

D: Applying stateful packet inspection to detect and allow only HTTP traffic on port 80 and 443

Correct Answer: A

Explanation: Enabling a firewall rule that specifically allows only TCP port 80 through the VPN tunnel ensures that only HTTP traffic is allowed. This configuration limits the traffic passing through the VPN, protecting the internal network by restricting access to the specified web service.

----

196. Which firewall command should be used to block all incoming traffic from a specific IP address while allowing outgoing traffic to all destinations?

A: firewall-cmd --permanent --add-rich-rule 'rule family="ipv4" source address="192.168.1.100" reject'

B: ufw deny from 192.168.1.100

C: pfctl -t blocklist -T add 192.168.1.100

D: iptables -A INPUT -s 192.168.1.100 -j DROP

Correct Answer: D
Explanation: The iptables -A INPUT command is used to add a rule that drops incoming traffic from a specific IP address, while allowing other traffic to pass. This is effective in scenarios where you want to block malicious sources but allow regular outgoing traffic.

----

197. When configuring an IDS/IPS solution to monitor traffic for specific types of attacks, which step should be taken to ensure that it detects suspicious patterns in encrypted network traffic?

A: Relying on flow-based detection to monitor traffic streams and identify encrypted threats without deep inspection

B: Configuring the IDS/IPS to rely on heuristic analysis for encrypted traffic, identifying malicious behavior based on statistical anomalies

C: Using a passive network tap to capture traffic and analyze it with pattern-matching algorithms

D: Enabling SSL/TLS termination on a dedicated proxy to inspect encrypted traffic for malicious patterns

Correct Answer: D
Explanation: Enabling SSL/TLS termination on a proxy server allows the IDS/IPS to inspect the decrypted traffic before it is re-encrypted for transmission to the internal network. This ensures that encrypted attacks can be detected by analyzing the unencrypted traffic.

----

198. Fill in the blank: In a firewall configuration, creating a rule to allow incoming HTTP traffic requires opening _____.

A: TCP port 22

B: UDP port 161

C: UDP port 53

D: TCP port 80

Correct Answer: D
Explanation: Opening TCP port 80 is necessary for HTTP traffic, as this port is commonly used for web services. Configuring the firewall to allow this port ensures that incoming web requests can reach the server, while other ports can remain blocked for security.

----

199. A security team wants to prevent SQL injection attacks from reaching their internal database server. What should be configured on the firewall to ensure this?

A: Setting deep packet inspection rules to detect SQL queries and block malicious patterns before they reach the database server

B: Setting up whitelists of allowed SQL commands and blocking any queries that deviate from the norm

C: Using NAT rules to redirect incoming queries to a security appliance that checks for SQL injection attacks

D: Applying generic firewall rules that block all SQL traffic to the database server, regardless of the query's source

Correct Answer: A
Explanation: Deep packet inspection (DPI) allows the firewall to analyze the payload of network packets for specific malicious content, such as SQL injection patterns. By blocking such patterns, the firewall prevents these attacks from reaching the internal database server.

----

200. An administrator is implementing an IPS to actively block known malicious traffic. What configuration would best ensure that the system blocks attacks without affecting normal traffic flow?

A: Using deep learning algorithms to block emerging threats based on abnormal traffic patterns

B: Applying behavior-based traffic analysis to block abnormal traffic without identifying known signatures

C: Configuring signature-based detection to block traffic matching specific known attack patterns without scanning benign traffic

D: Enforcing rate-limiting rules to block excessive traffic from specific IP addresses that exhibit malicious behavior

Correct Answer: C

Explanation: Signature-based detection is ideal for an IPS, as it blocks traffic that matches known attack signatures while allowing normal traffic to pass. This approach ensures minimal disruption to regular network traffic, focusing only on malicious patterns.

----

201. A SOC analyst needs to configure a network monitoring tool to filter out false positives related to common web traffic on port 443. What rule should they apply to achieve this without missing genuine threats?

A: Set a threshold for alerts on any traffic over 100 MB/s, as this is likely to be an intrusion.

B: Exclude all HTTPS traffic from the monitoring scope to reduce the volume of logged data.

C: Implement a complete block on all traffic to and from the port, ensuring no data breaches occur.

D: Adjust the SIEM system to increase sensitivity to anomalies while excluding typical data patterns associated with SSL/TLS encrypted data.

Correct Answer: D
Explanation: The correct rule maximizes the effectiveness of monitoring by focusing on deviations from normal encrypted web traffic patterns without ignoring other anomalies, thus maintaining a balance between usability and security.

----

202. In incident response, determining the root cause of an attack is crucial. What command can be used in a Unix-based system to review chronological system events that could indicate the initial breach point?

A: Use the netstat command to check active connections and listening ports on the system.

B: Run the top command to identify and monitor real-time processes consuming high system resources.

C: Use the zgrep command to filter and search compressed log files for specific error codes or login attempts.

D: Execute the last command to display the most recent user logins and their originating IP addresses.

Correct Answer: C
Explanation: zgrep allows for efficient analysis of compressed logs to backtrack and pinpoint events leading up to the security incident, providing valuable insights into the timeline of the attack.

----

203. Fill in the blank: To ensure that security alerts are effectively escalated, a SOC must maintain a(n) _____ that outlines steps to be taken when specific types of alerts are received.
A: "Incident Response Plan" (IRP)

B: "Communications Protocol" (CP)

C: "Alert Escalation Policy" (AEP)

D: "Standard Operating Procedure" (SOP)

Correct Answer: D
Explanation: A Standard Operating Procedure helps in standardizing the response process across the SOC, ensuring that each type of alert is handled consistently and effectively according to predefined protocols.

----

204. During a typical day, a SOC analyst observes unusual outbound traffic from a supposedly secure server. The analyst needs to quickly assess whether this is a routine update or an exfiltration attempt. Which of the following is the most critical first step?
A: Perform a network sweep to identify all active connections to and from the server.

B: Verify the authenticity of the server's SSL certificate to rule out a man-in-the-middle attack masquerading as normal traffic.

C: Check the server's recent patch history to determine if a scheduled update was applied.

D: Initiate a rollback of the server to its most recent secure state before the traffic anomaly was detected.

Correct Answer: B
Explanation: Verifying the SSL certificate first helps confirm whether the communication is secure and genuine or compromised, which is crucial in determining the nature of the unexpected traffic.

----

205. An experienced SOC analyst is conducting a training session on recognizing signs of potential data breaches. What scenario should they use to demonstrate how to identify a subtle, yet significant, security threat?
A: Describe an attack where multiple employee credentials are used simultaneously from geographically disparate locations.

B: A scenario where small, intermittent data transfers occur at irregular intervals, possibly during off-hours, to avoid detection.

C: A situation where a large number of failed login attempts is detected on an administrative account during a weekend.

D: Outline a phishing attack that involves a seemingly legitimate email requesting sensitive information.

Correct Answer: B

Explanation: This scenario teaches analysts to recognize and investigate smaller data movements that could indicate data exfiltration, which often go unnoticed in favor of larger, more obvious transfers.

----

206. What command would you use to display all network connections, listening ports, and routing tables in a Windows environment to monitor suspicious activities?

A: Use the netstat -an command to view all network connections, listening ports, and the routing table, essential for identifying unauthorized connections.

B: Apply the tracert -d command to trace the route packets take to a network host, providing insights into the path and potential delays.

C: Launch the ping -t command to continuously send echo requests to a host, monitoring network connectivity and response time.

D: Execute the ipconfig /displaydns command to show all the DNS cache entries, which can reveal recently accessed internet locations.

Correct Answer: A

Explanation: The netstat -an command provides comprehensive information on network connections and routing, which is crucial for monitoring and diagnosing network issues and ensuring that no unauthorized connections have been established.

----

207. A cybersecurity technician needs to set up an IDS to monitor network traffic on a Linux server. What is the command to mirror traffic from eth0 to eth1 for monitoring purposes?

A: Use sudo iptables -A FORWARD -i eth0 -o eth1 -j ACCEPT to forward all traffic from eth0 to eth1 directly.

B: Implement echo 1 > /proc/sys/net/ipv4/ip_forward to enable packet forwarding through the Linux kernel.

C: Enter the command sudo tcpreplay --intf1=eth0 --intf2=eth1 capture.pcap to mirror packet data from one interface to another.

D: Configure sudo modprobe iptable_mirror to initiate traffic mirroring between two network interfaces.

Explanation: sudo tcpreplay is effective for mirroring traffic between interfaces, allowing for detailed analysis and monitoring of network traffic, crucial for intrusion detection systems.

----

208. Fill in the blank: The most effective tool for visualizing real-time data traffic and pinpointing anomalies in a large corporate network is a _____.

A: "Network traffic analyzer"

B: "Automated threat detection system"

C: "Comprehensive logging suite"

D: "Protocol analyzer"

Explanation: Network traffic analyzers are essential tools for real-time monitoring and analyzing network traffic, helping detect, diagnose, and respond to anomalies effectively.

----

209. An analyst notices an anomaly in traffic patterns on a network monitoring dashboard. What should be the first step in investigating this anomaly?

A: Conduct a physical inspection of all network hardware involved in the traffic anomaly to check for unauthorized devices.

B: Escalate the issue to the senior network administrator before taking any steps to understand or mitigate the traffic anomaly.

C: Review the detailed logs provided by the network monitoring tools to identify the source and nature of the traffic anomaly.

D: Immediately isolate the affected network segment to prevent potential spread of malicious activity.

Explanation: Reviewing logs is a fundamental first step in investigating network anomalies, as it allows the analyst to understand the context and specifics of the traffic spike or pattern, aiding in rapid diagnosis and response.

----

210. When configuring a network monitoring tool on a Linux server, which command ensures continuous capture of packet data that matches a specific pattern?

A: Run the nmap -p 80 --script http-headers 192.168.1.1 to scan for HTTP headers from a given IP, indicating web server configurations and activity.

B: Execute ifconfig eth0 promisc to put the network interface in promiscuous mode, allowing it to intercept and log all network packets.

C: Implement the tcpdump -i eth0 'host 192.168.1.1 and port 80' -w output.pcap -C 100 to continuously monitor traffic from a specific IP and port, saving it in manageable files.

D: Use the wireshark -k -i eth0 -f "host 192.168.1.1 and port 80" to graphically analyze and log network traffic from a specific host and port.

Correct Answer: C

Explanation: The tcpdump command with specified IP and port filtering and segmented output allows for efficient and targeted monitoring of network traffic, facilitating quick identification of issues or threats without overwhelming the storage with excessive data.

----

211. In setting up a centralized logging solution for a corporate network, which configuration directive should be used within rsyslog to forward all logs to a central log server?

A: Set *.* @remote-host:514 to forward logs to a specified remote host over UDP.

B: Configure $template DynaFile,"/var/log/%HOSTNAME%/%PROGRAMNAME%.log" for dynamic file path generation based on the source hostname.

C: Apply *.* @@remote-syslog-server for secure log transmission using TLS encryption to a remote syslog server.

D: Use $ModLoad imtcp; $InputTCPServerRun 514 to enable TCP input module and listen on the standard syslog port.

Correct Answer: D

Explanation: Enabling TCP input and setting the server to listen on the syslog port are crucial for a secure and reliable centralized logging system, allowing for robust log collection without the unreliability of UDP.

----

212. What command would a cybersecurity technician use to verify the integrity of log files stored on a Linux server, ensuring they have not been tampered with?

A: Use md5sum /path/to/logfile | compare /path/to/previous-md5 to check for any changes in the file since the last checksum.

B: Execute sha256sum -c /path/to/logfile.sha256 to check the hash against the stored value and ensure log file integrity.

C: Deploy grep 'ERROR' /path/to/logfile to search for error messages that might indicate tampering or system issues.

D: Run ls -l /path/to/logfile to verify file permissions and ownership, checking for unauthorized changes.

Correct Answer: B
Explanation: Using sha256sum -c provides a straightforward and highly reliable method to verify the integrity of log files by comparing their current hash to a previously calculated hash, ensuring logs have not been altered.

----

213. Fill in the blank: For automated analysis of security logs to identify patterns indicating a potential security breach, most companies implement a

_____.

A: "Automated log parsing and alerting tool"

B: "Security Information and Event Management (SIEM) system"

C: "Distributed denial of service (DDoS) prevention system"

D: "Advanced persistent threat (APT) detection tool"

Correct Answer: B
Explanation: SIEM systems are integral to modern security operations, providing real-time analysis of security alerts generated by network hardware and applications, and are essential for detecting subtle patterns that indicate security incidents.

----

214. During a review of network logs, a security analyst notices an anomaly in HTTP request methods. What should be the analyst's first action to investigate this issue?

A: Isolate the server receiving the suspicious HTTP requests to prevent any potential impact on the rest of the network.

B: Correlate the suspicious request methods with known attack vectors to determine if it is part of a known exploit or attack.

C: Update firewall rules to block the source IP address associated with the anomalous HTTP requests immediately.

D: Consult with other team members to get a consensus on whether the traffic pattern is normal for this server.

Correct Answer: B
Explanation: Analyzing suspicious request methods against known attack patterns allows the analyst to quickly assess the nature of the anomaly and respond appropriately, which is vital for mitigating potential threats.

----

215. When configuring a log management solution to ensure compliance with data protection regulations, which factor is most crucial for configuring log retention policies?

A: Establish a routine for regularly auditing the log management system to ensure it functions correctly and efficiently.

B: Ensure that logs are retained for the minimum required duration specified by relevant legal or regulatory standards.

C: Implement encryption of log files to protect the data from unauthorized access during transmission and storage.

D: Focus on optimizing log rotation settings to manage storage space effectively while maintaining access to old logs.

Correct Answer: B
Explanation: Adhering to legal and regulatory requirements for log retention is critical to ensure compliance and avoid legal issues, making it the most important factor in setting up log retention policies in a compliance-driven environment.

----

216. To configure an IDS to detect SQL injection attempts, which Snort rule should be used?

A: Use alert icmp $EXTERNAL_NET any -> $HOME_NET any (msg:"ICMP Traffic"; itype:8; sid:1000005; rev:1;) to monitor unexpected ICMP traffic.

B: Deploy alert udp $EXTERNAL_NET any -> $HOME_NET 53 (msg:"DNS Tunneling Detected"; content:"|00 ff|"; sid:1000020; rev:1;) for detecting DNS tunneling activities.

C: Apply alert tcp $EXTERNAL_NET any -> $HOME_NET 3306 (msg:"SQL Injection Attempt"; content:"select"; nocase; content:"drop"; distance:0; within:40; sid:1000004; rev:1;) to detect common SQL keywords misuse.

D: Set log tcp $EXTERNAL_NET any -> $HOME_NET 1433 (msg:"Potential MSSQL Attack"; flow:to_server,established; content:"xp_"; sid:1000010; rev:1;) to identify possible attacks on MSSQL databases.

Correct Answer: C
Explanation: This Snort rule is precisely formulated to capture the essence of an SQL injection attack by looking for suspicious SQL commands within the payload, which are indicative of malicious attempts to manipulate databases.

----

217. What is the essential command to update the rule set for an open-source IDS like Snort on a Linux system?

A: Run sudo apt-get install --only-upgrade snort to ensure the IDS is running the latest software version.

B: Utilize snort -V to verify the current version and manually download rule updates if necessary.

C: Execute sudo snort -u snort -g snort -c /etc/snort/snort.conf --update-rules to fetch and apply the latest IDS rules.

D: Implement snort -R /path/to/custom.rules to reload custom rules without updating the entire rule set.

Correct Answer: C
Explanation: Using the specified command ensures that Snort's rule set is up to date, critical for maintaining the effectiveness of the IDS against new and evolving threats.

----

218. Fill in the blank: The most effective IDS for detecting anomalies based on network behavior is referred to as a(n) _____.

A: "Behavioral Intrusion Detection System" (BIDS)

B: "Host-based Intrusion Detection System" (HBIDS)

C: "Signature-based Intrusion Detection System" (SBIDS)

D: "Network-based Intrusion Detection System" (NBIDS)

Correct Answer: A

Explanation: A Behavioral Intrusion Detection System excels in identifying anomalies by analyzing the behavior of the network traffic, which is crucial for detecting sophisticated threats that do not match known signatures.

----

219. A cybersecurity technician observes multiple failed login attempts followed by a successful login from the same IP. What is the initial step in investigating this using IDS logs?

A: Review firewall logs to identify if the IP should be blocked or further monitored for suspicious activity.

B: Conduct a detailed user behavior analysis for that IP over the last 24 hours to determine typical activity patterns.

C: Analyze the sequence of failed attempts to establish if the successful login was a brute force attack result.

D: Immediately reset the user account password and review recent activity to ensure no unauthorized actions were taken.

Correct Answer: C

Explanation: Analyzing the sequence and timing of failed attempts followed by a success can reveal patterns typical of brute force attacks, allowing for immediate and targeted response measures.

----

220. When setting up IDS to monitor encrypted traffic, what is the necessary configuration to decrypt SSL/TLS traffic for analysis without compromising security?

A: Configure a dedicated SSL proxy to handle decryption and re-encryption separately before passing traffic to the IDS.

B: Implement inline decryption with ssl_bump directive in Squid to allow IDS to inspect the plaintext traffic without exposing private keys.

C: Enable TLS decryption at the IDS level by integrating with a network HSM to securely manage and apply cryptographic keys.

D: Use stunnel on both ends of the connection to decrypt and re-encrypt traffic transparently to the IDS.

Correct Answer: B
Explanation: The ssl_bump directive in Squid provides a method to transparently decrypt and inspect SSL/TLS traffic, crucial for IDS to perform deep packet inspection on encrypted flows while ensuring the encryption keys remain secure.

----

221. What configuration command should be used to enable automatic blocking of suspicious IP addresses on a Cisco IPS device?

A: Enable ip inspect name mymap tcp to inspect and automatically block suspicious TCP traffic.

B: Set auto shun to automatically shun hosts that are identified as sources of attack traffic.

C: Activate intrusion-prevention active mode to engage real-time traffic analysis and blocking of attacks.

D: Use ip ips deny-action ips-interface to configure the IPS to automatically block traffic from detected malicious sources.

Correct Answer: D
Explanation: The command ip ips deny-action ips-interface enables the IPS to take immediate action against identified threats by blocking traffic from suspicious IPs, crucial for preventing potential intrusions before they harm the network.

----

222. To enhance an IPS with the capability to stop zero-day exploits, which technology should it be integrated with?

A: Integrate the IPS with a threat intelligence platform that provides real-time updates about emerging threats.

B: Enhance the IPS by incorporating an AI-driven anomaly detection system that learns from network behavior.

C: Combine the IPS with advanced malware protection (AMP) to block unknown malware based on behavioral analysis.

D: Link the IPS with a sandboxing tool that isolates and analyzes suspicious files in a safe environment.

Correct Answer: A
Explanation: Integrating with a threat intelligence platform allows the IPS to utilize up-to-date information about emerging threats, enhancing its ability to preemptively block attacks, including zero-day exploits.

----

223. Fill in the blank: To maximize the effectiveness of an IPS in a distributed enterprise environment, it should be configured for _____.

A: "centralized management"

B: "segmented control"

C: "redundant installations"

D: "automated response protocols"

Correct Answer: A

Explanation: Centralized management of an IPS ensures that security policies and configurations are consistently applied across the entire distributed network, simplifying monitoring and management while enhancing security response capabilities.

----

224. In a simulated attack scenario, an IPS is set to detect and block a ransomware payload from entering the network. What should be the first action once the IPS alerts on the payload?

A: Isolate the network segment where the alert was generated to prevent further spread of potential ransomware.

B: Verify the alert's authenticity and examine the payload signature to ensure it matches known threat patterns.

C: Immediately notify cybersecurity incident response teams to initiate a company-wide security audit.

D: Conduct a network sweep to identify any other instances of the malware that may have bypassed the IPS.

Correct Answer: B

Explanation: Verifying the authenticity of an alert and examining the signature of the payload are vital first steps to confirm the detection is accurate and to determine the appropriate response, minimizing false positives and ensuring real threats are addressed promptly.

----

225. For an IPS managing encrypted traffic, what configuration ensures that traffic remains secure while enabling effective intrusion prevention?

A: Set up a dedicated proxy server to decrypt all incoming and outgoing traffic, independently analyzing it before re-encryption.

B: Configure the IPS to work in conjunction with a network-based decryption appliance that handles TLS/SSL before passing traffic to the IPS.

C: Utilize endpoint protection platforms (EPP) to decrypt traffic on the host machines, offloading this task from the IPS.

D: Implement strict access control lists (ACLs) that filter encrypted traffic based on source and destination IPs.

Correct Answer: B
Explanation: Using a network-based decryption appliance in conjunction with the IPS allows encrypted traffic to be inspected without compromising the security of the encryption, maintaining data privacy while still enabling effective intrusion prevention.

----

226. What command is used to view the current status and configuration of the SIEM agent installed on a Linux server?
A: Use tail -f /var/log/siemagent.log to continuously monitor the SIEM agent's activity log for real-time troubleshooting.

B: Apply grep 'ERROR' /var/log/siemagent.log to search for recent error messages related to the SIEM agent's operations.

C: Run systemctl status siem.service to obtain detailed service information and error logs for the SIEM system.

D: Execute sudo /etc/init.d/siemagent status to check the operational status and basic settings of the SIEM agent.

Correct Answer: D
Explanation: The sudo /etc/init.d/siemagent status command provides a quick and straightforward method to verify the SIEM agent's status and configuration on a Linux server, ensuring it is operational and configured correctly.

----

227. A SIEM solution must be configured to automate alerts for which type of security event that typically indicates a brute force attack?
A: Set alert rules to trigger when multiple failed login attempts are detected from the same IP address within a short time frame.

B: Configure the system to send an alert when an unusually high number of file deletion events occurs.

C: Enable notifications for changes in user privileges or group memberships that occur without prior approval.

D: Alert administrators when encryption protocols are changed or certificates are updated on critical servers.

Correct Answer: A

Explanation: Configuring SIEM to alert on multiple failed logins from the same IP effectively identifies potential brute force attacks, allowing for rapid response and mitigation, crucial for maintaining security.

----

228. Fill in the blank: The key component of SIEM that allows for the real-time visualization of security data is known as a _____.

A: "dashboard"

B: "analytical engine"

C: "data parser"

D: "log collector"

Correct Answer: A

Explanation: A dashboard is essential in SIEM for providing a centralized, real-time visual representation of security events and data, enabling immediate analysis and quicker decision-making during security incidents.

----

229. During a compliance audit, it is discovered that not all endpoint security logs are being transmitted to the SIEM. What is the first action to rectify this issue?

A: Manually force a log synchronization for all endpoints from the central SIEM console to confirm log receipt.

B: Verify network connectivity and permissions for the affected endpoints to ensure they can communicate with the SIEM.

C: Reinstall the endpoint security solutions to ensure they are properly integrated with the SIEM's logging functions.

D: Update the SIEM software to the latest version, hoping to resolve any compatibility issues with newer endpoint agents.

Correct Answer: B

Explanation: Ensuring that network connectivity and permissions are correctly configured for endpoints addresses common issues that can prevent logs from being transmitted to SIEM, essential for comprehensive security event management.

---

230. How should a SIEM be configured to handle an influx of log data during a major network incident without losing any critical information?

A: Temporarily reduce the detail level of logs to prevent the SIEM from being overwhelmed by less significant data.

B: Enable a cloud-based overflow service for log storage that automatically activates during high traffic periods.

C: Increase the SIEM's log storage capacity and adjust the event correlation settings to prioritize critical events.

D: Implement a secondary SIEM system to create a redundant log management environment.

Correct Answer: C

Explanation: Increasing log storage capacity and refining event correlation settings during significant network incidents ensure that all critical information is captured and prioritized, maintaining the integrity and utility of the security data collected.

---

231. What is the most effective method for configuring a UBA system to detect unauthorized access to confidential files?

A: Require multi-factor authentication for all users when accessing sensitive documents, regardless of the time or location.

B: Automatically block user access to sensitive files if they are accessed during non-business hours.

C: Configure the UBA to alert when a user accesses files outside of their normal working hours or from unusual IP addresses.

D: Set the UBA to monitor all file access events and flag any that involve encrypted files or external devices.

Correct Answer: C

Explanation: Configuring alerts for file access outside of normal working hours or from unusual IP addresses efficiently targets the specific vectors through which unauthorized access typically occurs, leveraging UBA's strength in monitoring for deviations from established user patterns.

---

232. In User Behavior Analytics, what statistical model is typically used to identify anomalies in user activity patterns?

A: Apply cluster analysis to group similar user activities and highlight any that fall outside the clusters.

B: Utilize neural networks to identify complex patterns in user behavior that may indicate sophisticated threats.

C: Employ a Bayesian statistical model to calculate the probability of various user actions based on historical data.

D: Use a regression analysis model to trend user behavior over time and spot outliers.

Correct Answer: C
Explanation: A Bayesian model is well-suited for UBA as it provides a probabilistic approach that evaluates the likelihood of user actions based on accumulated data, making it highly effective for spotting activities that diverge from established norms.

----

233. Fill in the blank: To enhance the detection of insider threats, UBA systems commonly integrate with _____ to monitor real-time user activities and network traffic.

A: "Security Information and Event Management (SIEM) systems"

B: "Endpoint Detection and Response (EDR) solutions"

C: "Advanced Threat Protection (ATP) services"

D: "Data Loss Prevention (DLP) tools"

Correct Answer: A
Explanation: Integrating UBA with SIEM enhances threat detection capabilities by combining user behavior analysis with event and log data, providing a holistic view of security events that aids in detecting and responding to insider threats more effectively.

----

234. An analyst finds unusual login times and location changes in a user's activity. What should be the first step in investigating these anomalies using UBA tools?

A: Launch an audit of the user's email and communication logs to check for any data exfiltration attempts.

B: Correlate the unusual activities with recent changes in the user's role or permission settings.

C: Notify the cybersecurity response team to conduct an immediate investigation into the potential security breach.

D: Immediately revoke the user's access privileges until the behavior can be verified as legitimate or malicious.

Correct Answer: B
Explanation: Examining correlations between unusual activity and changes in a user's role or permissions can clarify whether such activity might be legitimate, thereby refining the investigation process and focusing efforts where they are most needed.

----

235. How should a UBA system be configured to ensure it accurately identifies deviations from a user's typical behavior without generating excessive false positives?

A: Increase the logging detail of user activities to provide more data points for anomaly detection.

B: Employ a rule-based system where specific user actions under certain conditions are flagged as suspicious.

C: Set thresholds based on statistical averages of user behavior over a defined period, adjusting sensitivity based on the role.

D: Implement machine learning algorithms to dynamically adapt thresholds based on continuous user behavior analysis.

Correct Answer: C
Explanation: Setting behavior thresholds based on statistical analysis of user activity over time allows for personalized monitoring. Adjusting sensitivity according to the user's role accommodates different access needs and behavioral patterns, reducing false positives while still effectively identifying genuine anomalies.

----

236. Given the need to design a script that automates the response to detected network intrusions by isolating compromised systems, which command would be the most effective to include?

A: Update firewall rules with ufw deny from $HOST_IP to any

B: Launch a network scan using nmap -oG $HOST_IP -v

C: Initiate a system snapshot with rsync -a --delete /backup/ /$HOST_IP/

D: Terminate the session using the command iptables -A INPUT -s $HOST_IP -j DROP

Correct Answer: D

Explanation: The command iptables -A INPUT -s $HOST_IP -j DROP effectively isolates a compromised system by immediately blocking all incoming traffic from its IP address, which is crucial for containing the threat and preventing further network intrusion.

----

237. When configuring a Security Information and Event Management (SIEM) system, what is the most crucial automated response feature to enable first for handling high-priority alerts?

A: Establish automated log archival

B: Enable real-time event correlation and alert prioritization

C: Set alerts for unauthorized access attempts

D: Configure automated backup for system logs

Correct Answer: B

Explanation: Enabling real-time event correlation and alert prioritization is essential as it allows the SIEM system to quickly identify and respond to the most critical threats based on predefined rules, enhancing the effectiveness of automated security responses.

----

238. Fill in the blank: To automate the process of applying patches to multiple systems simultaneously following a vulnerability alert, the _____ tool is typically used.

A: Ansible

B: Chef

C: SaltStack

D: Puppet

Correct Answer: A

Explanation: Ansible is widely used for its ability to handle complex batch jobs across multiple systems, making it suitable for automating the patching process in response to security alerts, thereby ensuring that all targeted systems are updated simultaneously to address any identified vulnerabilities efficiently.

----

239. In a simulated cyber attack scenario, you are tasked to automatically disable user accounts exhibiting suspicious behavior. Which configuration command ensures this action is taken?

A: Configure audit logging with auditctl -w /var/log/auth.log -p wa -k user_activity

B: Apply a temporary IP block using iptables -A INPUT -s $HOST_IP -j DROP

C: Set the security policy to usermod -L $USER

D: Reinforce password policies with passwd -l $USER

Correct Answer: C

Explanation: The command usermod -L $USER locks a suspicious user's account, which is a direct and effective response to immediately stop any potential harmful actions by the user, securing the system against further unauthorized activities.

----

240. Analyze this scenario: Your organization's security automation tool is configured to trigger specific actions based on the severity of threats. For a medium severity threat, what is the most appropriate automated response?

A: Quarantine the affected system for further analysis

B: Redirect all traffic from the affected source to a honeypot

C: Implement automatic email notifications to the security team

D: Block the IP address related to the incident

Correct Answer: C

Explanation: Automatic email notifications provide a timely and efficient method for the security team to be alerted about medium severity threats, allowing them to quickly assess and address potential impacts without automatically taking drastic measures that might interrupt business operations.

----

241. What command would you use to scan for vulnerabilities on a network where Windows machines are predominant?

A: Deploy a script netstat -tuln | grep LISTEN to check open ports

B: Begin port forwarding with iptables -t nat -A PREROUTING -p tcp --dport 80 -j REDIRECT --to-port 8080

C: Use nmap -Pn --script vuln $TARGET_IP to perform the scan

D: Initiate a firewall rule update with sudo ufw allow from $SAFE_IP

Correct Answer: C
Explanation: The command nmap -Pn --script vuln $TARGET_IP is specifically designed to identify vulnerabilities in network services and software by using the Nmap Scripting Engine targeted at common vulnerabilities, which makes it highly suitable for scanning Windows machines that might be running a variety of services.

----

242. Fill in the blank: For regular vulnerability scanning of a web server, the most commonly used automated tool is _____.
A: Qualys

B: Nessus

C: OpenVAS

D: Burp Suite

Correct Answer: B
Explanation: Nessus is a robust vulnerability scanning tool that automates the process of checking for vulnerabilities and misconfigurations in web servers, making it a staple in many cybersecurity arsenals for its comprehensive testing capabilities that align with industry best practices.

----

243. When configuring a system to automatically update its security patches, what is the primary command to enable this feature on a Linux server?
A: Execute sudo apt-get update && sudo apt-get upgrade -y

B: Implement cron job for yum update

C: Set up auto-apt to handle automatic updates

D: Use dpkg --configure -a to ensure all packages are correctly installed

Correct Answer: A
Explanation: The command sudo apt-get update && sudo apt-get upgrade -y is critical for Linux servers as it ensures all the available updates and security patches are installed automatically. This command first updates the list of available packages and then upgrades them, applying any security patches without requiring user interaction during the process.

----

244. In a scenario where you need to prioritize patches after a vulnerability scan, which factor is most crucial for determining which patches to apply first?

A: Severity of the vulnerabilities reported

B: Cost of deployment per patch

C: Number of systems affected

D: Time required for patch implementation

Correct Answer: A

Explanation: Prioritizing patches based on the severity of the vulnerabilities reported is crucial because it allows security teams to address the most critical vulnerabilities that could potentially have the highest impact on the organization's security posture, thereby reducing the likelihood of exploitation.

----

245. Your company uses a centralized patch management system. What is the first step in ensuring that newly identified vulnerabilities are addressed in the next update cycle?

A: Update firewall settings to minimize network exposure during updates

B: Configure the system to alert users about the required restart

C: Review the latest vulnerability scan report for priority issues

D: Set a fixed schedule for system reboots after patching

Correct Answer: C

Explanation: Reviewing the latest vulnerability scan report for priority issues is essential in a centralized patch management system to ensure that the most critical vulnerabilities are identified and prioritized in the patch management cycle. This step helps in aligning the patching efforts with the current threat landscape and vulnerability exposure of the organization.

----

246. Which command would you run to ensure that all installed packages on a Linux server are up-to-date and any security patches are applied automatically?

A: Launch the process with dpkg --list | grep update

B: Use dnf update --security

C: Execute yum check-update --security

D: Run sudo apt-get update && sudo apt-get upgrade -y

Correct Answer: D

Explanation: Running sudo apt-get update && sudo apt-get upgrade -y ensures that all package lists are updated and that the latest versions of all packages are installed, including any critical security patches. This command allows for both updating package information and applying patches without requiring further user input, which is essential for keeping systems secure automatically.

----

247. Fill in the blank: To automate patch management across multiple Windows systems, a commonly used tool that integrates with PowerShell scripts is _____.

A: Ansible Playbooks

B: WSUS (Windows Server Update Services)

C: SCCM (System Center Configuration Manager)

D: Puppet automation

Correct Answer: B

Explanation: WSUS is a widely used tool for automating patch management in Windows environments, allowing administrators to control the distribution of updates released by Microsoft. It integrates well with PowerShell scripts, making it a flexible solution for managing updates across multiple Windows systems.

----

248. You are tasked with setting up a scheduled task to check for system updates and apply patches automatically. Which configuration command should you use on a Linux server to ensure that updates are applied daily without user intervention?

A: Use cron job to execute apt-get upgrade daily

B: Configure auto-patch system for weekly updates

C: Install auto-updater package with daily schedule

D: Schedule daily update checks via systemctl

Correct Answer: A

Explanation: A cron job to execute apt-get upgrade daily is a reliable way to automate the process of applying patches and updates on a Linux system without requiring user intervention. This ensures that the system regularly checks for updates and applies them automatically on a daily schedule, improving the security and stability of the system.

----

249. In a scenario where critical patches are available but have not yet been applied, what is the most appropriate automated action to configure in the system to ensure immediate patch application without manual approval?

A: Set alerts to notify administrators when patches are available

B: Disable auto-updates and require manual approval for all patches

C: Implement a restart policy that requires user approval

D: Set the update policy to auto-approve and auto-install

Correct Answer: D
Explanation: Configuring an update policy to auto-approve and auto-install allows the system to apply critical patches as soon as they become available, ensuring that vulnerabilities are addressed immediately. This configuration minimizes the risk of exploitation by applying patches without waiting for manual approval, which could delay protection.

----

250. A company wants to reduce downtime by applying patches in non-peak hours. What automated feature can be configured in the patch management system to ensure patches are applied during the specified maintenance window?

A: Implement a delay in patch deployment to minimize system disruption

B: Configure a maintenance window in the patching system for after hours

C: Limit patch installation to low-priority systems first

D: Set a time limit for installing patches to avoid reboots during work hours

Correct Answer: B
Explanation: Configuring a maintenance window in the patching system for after hours ensures that patches are applied during periods of low activity, reducing the impact on business operations. This feature allows organizations to apply updates while avoiding disruptions during peak working hours, thus balancing security needs with business continuity.

----

251. Which command can be used to list all currently installed software packages on a Linux machine for asset management purposes?

A: Execute rpm -qa to list all installed RPM packages

B: Use yum list installed to show all installed packages

C: Run dpkg --get-selections to list all installed packages

D: Issue apt list --installed to display the installed software packages

Correct Answer: C

Explanation: Running dpkg --get-selections on a Linux system provides a comprehensive list of all installed packages. This command is particularly useful for asset management as it gives an accurate and detailed report of all software currently on the system, which is essential for tracking and maintaining software inventories.

----

252. Fill in the blank: To automate the tracking and auditing of hardware assets in a network environment, _____ is commonly deployed to regularly scan devices.

A: Spiceworks Inventory

B: SolarWinds Network Performance Monitor

C: Nagios XI

D: ManageEngine Asset Explorer

Correct Answer: B

Explanation: SolarWinds Network Performance Monitor offers advanced device tracking and scanning capabilities, making it ideal for automating hardware asset audits across large networks. Its ability to detect, monitor, and report on devices ensures that all hardware assets are accurately tracked.

----

253. You are tasked with keeping an accurate inventory of all software assets across multiple systems. Which tool should you use to automate the process of discovering software installations across your organization?

A: Use a custom-built PowerShell script for auditing software installations

B: Utilize Microsoft System Center Configuration Manager (SCCM)

C: Integrate with Open Source Software Asset Management (OSSAM) tools

D: Run Windows Management Instrumentation (WMI) queries on each machine

Correct Answer: B
Explanation: Microsoft System Center Configuration Manager (SCCM) is highly effective for automating the discovery of software installations across multiple machines in an organization. It helps administrators maintain accurate inventories by automatically scanning and reporting on software assets.

----

254. In a scenario where a company needs to track newly added devices on their network, what is the best way to ensure that every new device is automatically logged into the asset management system?
A: Manually input new devices into the system upon discovery

B: Configure automatic device discovery in the asset management tool

C: Implement an approval process for adding devices to the network

D: Install an agent-based solution on all new devices

Correct Answer: B
Explanation: Configuring automatic device discovery in the asset management tool ensures that any new device added to the network is automatically detected and logged. This prevents any manual tracking errors and maintains a current and up-to-date asset inventory without requiring user intervention.

----

255. Your organization needs to regularly audit hardware resources such as CPU, memory, and storage on all servers. What configuration should you use to automatically gather and report hardware changes on a weekly basis?
A: Deploy an SNMP server to monitor hardware changes

B: Leverage Puppet automation to handle hardware asset audits

C: Configure an Ansible playbook to capture hardware information weekly

D: Set up cron job to execute lshw every week

Correct Answer: D
Explanation: Setting up a cron job to execute lshw on a weekly basis provides an automated way to gather detailed hardware information such as CPU, memory, and storage on all servers. This scheduled task ensures that any hardware changes are tracked and reported regularly, facilitating efficient asset management practices.

---

256. Which command would you use to gather information about open ports and services running on a target IP address for threat intelligence purposes?

A: Launch ping $TARGET_IP to test connectivity and gather latency information

B: Use nmap -sV $TARGET_IP to identify open ports and services

C: Run netstat -an to list active connections and listening ports

D: Initiate traceroute $TARGET_IP to track the route to the target server

Correct Answer: B

Explanation: The nmap -sV $TARGET_IP command is essential for gathering detailed information about open ports and services on a target IP address, which helps in identifying potential vulnerabilities and entry points for attackers. This data is critical in building a comprehensive threat intelligence profile of the target, allowing security teams to better assess the threat landscape.

---

257. Fill in the blank: The most effective way to automate gathering threat intelligence data from multiple sources in real-time is by integrating _____ into the security operations center's workflow.

A: Threat intelligence platform (TIP)

B: Web scraping automation for threat reports

C: Real-time feed integration in the SIEM

D: Anomaly detection engine to flag abnormal behavior

Correct Answer: A

Explanation: A threat intelligence platform (TIP) automates the collection, aggregation, and analysis of threat data from various sources. Integrating a TIP into the security operations workflow allows for real-time correlation of threat intelligence across different feeds, which enhances the ability to detect, prioritize, and respond to threats quickly and efficiently.

---

258. You are tasked with monitoring for potential Indicators of Compromise (IOCs) on a network. What tool should you configure to continuously gather threat intelligence and alert you when specific IOCs are detected?

A: Install IDS/IPS and set up alert triggers for suspicious traffic

B: Enable automated alerts for suspicious network traffic

C: Configure SIEM rules to trigger on IOC matches

D: Set up DNS filtering to block malicious domains automatically

Correct Answer: C
Explanation: Configuring SIEM rules to trigger on IOC matches ensures continuous monitoring of the network for potential threats. By setting specific rules to detect known indicators such as IP addresses, file hashes, or domain names associated with malware, the system can automatically alert the security team when a match is found, allowing for a faster response to emerging threats.

----

259. In a scenario where you need to analyze potential threats from an email phishing campaign, which action should be performed first to gather intelligence on the sender's IP and potential malicious attachments?
A: Set up a firewall rule to block emails from suspicious senders

B: Submit the suspicious email attachments to a sandbox for analysis

C: Use the email headers to extract and analyze the sender's IP address

D: Isolate the affected workstation for further investigation

Correct Answer: C
Explanation: Analyzing the email headers to extract and investigate the sender's IP address is the first step in gathering intelligence from a phishing email. This allows the security team to trace the origin of the attack and cross-reference the IP with threat intelligence databases to determine if the sender has been flagged for suspicious activities. Additionally, analyzing the attachments in a controlled environment helps uncover potential malware.

----

260. Your organization subscribes to several threat intelligence feeds. What configuration should you implement to ensure that the data from these feeds is properly parsed and categorized for use in your incident response system?
A: Use a Python script to categorize threat intelligence feed data

B: Integrate a threat intelligence API with automated parsing logic

C: Store all threat intelligence data in a secure offline repository for manual review

D: Configure log aggregation to parse incoming threat intelligence feeds

Explanation: Integrating a threat intelligence API with automated parsing logic ensures that the raw data from multiple feeds is transformed into actionable intelligence. This configuration allows for efficient categorization, filtering, and prioritization of the incoming threat data, enabling the incident response team to focus on the most relevant and critical threats first.

----

261. What command would you use to automatically isolate a compromised machine from the network using a SOAR platform during an active incident response process?

A: Run ufw deny from $COMPROMISED_IP to block access

B: Use the command iptables -A INPUT -s $COMPROMISED_IP -j DROP

C: Execute nmap -Pn $COMPROMISED_IP to detect live systems

D: Use netstat -an | grep $COMPROMISED_IP to list active connections

Correct Answer: B

Explanation: The command iptables -A INPUT -s $COMPROMISED_IP -j DROP effectively isolates a compromised machine from the network by blocking incoming traffic from its IP address. This is a critical response action that can be automated through SOAR platforms to immediately contain threats and prevent further damage.

----

262. Fill in the blank: A SOAR solution that integrates with a Security Information and Event Management (SIEM) system can trigger automated playbooks when specific alerts are generated by _____.

A: SIEM log ingestion services

B: Email security gateways for inbound traffic

C: User activity anomaly detection systems

D: Correlated threat intelligence feeds

Correct Answer: D

Explanation: Correlated threat intelligence feeds are essential for triggering automated playbooks in a SOAR system. By integrating with SIEM, a SOAR solution can act on real-time threat data, enabling automated incident responses whenever a specific security alert is triggered, improving reaction time and reducing manual efforts.

----

263. You need to create an automated workflow to respond to potential phishing attempts. Which configuration step should be included first to ensure that malicious emails are quarantined automatically?

A: Activate sandbox analysis for suspicious email attachments

B: Set up email filtering with automatic quarantine of flagged messages

C: Configure spam filtering to alert administrators

D: Implement content filtering to scan attachments for malware

Correct Answer: B
Explanation: Setting up email filtering with automatic quarantine of flagged messages ensures that phishing emails are immediately isolated and cannot reach their intended targets. This step is crucial in phishing incident response workflows as it prevents further compromise by containing the threat at its source.

----

264. In a scenario where a company wants to automatically block malicious IP addresses after detecting suspicious traffic, what would be the most effective SOAR configuration to implement for real-time threat response?

A: Deploy firewall policies to manually handle IP blocking

B: Configure IP blocking rules based on real-time threat detection

C: Set up manual intervention alerts for suspicious IP addresses

D: Set up real-time logging for IP address activity without automated blocking

Correct Answer: B
Explanation: Configuring IP blocking rules based on real-time threat detection is an effective way to automatically block malicious IP addresses. SOAR platforms can be set to trigger such actions when suspicious traffic is detected, ensuring an immediate response to prevent further attacks from the detected threat source.

----

265. Your organization wants to implement an automated process for handling low-level security incidents, such as failed login attempts. Which SOAR feature should be enabled to automatically classify and respond to these incidents without manual intervention?

A: Schedule recurring scans for low-level security events

B: Send notifications to the security team for each failed login attempt

C: Manually escalate low-priority incidents to the security operations team

D: Enable automatic incident classification based on severity levels

Correct Answer: D
Explanation: Enabling automatic incident classification based on severity levels allows a SOAR platform to handle low-level security incidents, such as failed login attempts, without requiring human intervention. This feature ensures that routine incidents are handled efficiently, freeing up security personnel to focus on more critical threats.

----

266. In configuring a UTM device to filter traffic and protect against web-based threats, which configuration command correctly sets up a rule to block access to known malicious URLs?

A: url-block list "dangerous_urls" action=block

B: set policy url-filtering block "malicious_sites"

C: set url access-group "malicious_sites" action=deny

D: apply filter access-list "bad_urls" deny

Correct Answer: B
Explanation: The correct command, set policy url-filtering block "malicious_sites", is specifically tailored for UTM devices to block traffic to URLs categorized as malicious based on updated databases. This command effectively enhances the security posture by preventing access to potentially harmful sites.

----

267. Which command should be used on a UTM appliance to implement a network rule that allows HTTP traffic from the internal network (192.168.1.0/24) to the Internet while ensuring deep packet inspection?

A: set network rule from=192.168.1.0/24 to=0.0.0.0/0 service=HTTP action=allow inspect=deep

B: rule add network=192.168.1.0/24 protocol=HTTP allow inspection=deep

C: implement rule http allow from net=192.168.1.0/24 deep-inspect

D: allow http from 192.168.1.0/24 inspect using dpi

Correct Answer: A
Explanation: The command set network rule from=192.168.1.0/24 to=0.0.0.0/0 service=HTTP action=allow inspect=deep is essential for allowing HTTP traffic from the

internal network while performing deep packet inspection to identify and block potential threats hidden in the traffic, maintaining robust perimeter defense.

----

268. Fill in the blank: To optimize the UTM performance by enabling caching of frequently accessed sites, the correct CLI command is _____.

A: cache enable site=frequent

B: enable cache optimization

C: activate http caching

D: set optimization cache-enabled

Correct Answer: B

Explanation: enable cache optimization is the direct command to turn on caching functionality in UTM devices. This enhances performance by storing copies of frequently requested web content, reducing latency and the load on the device's resources.

----

269. An organization is using a UTM appliance to consolidate security functions. If configuring the appliance to enforce anti-virus checking and spam filtering for email traffic, which command correctly sets up this dual function?

A: email security enable virus-scan spam-detect

B: set gateway smtp check-virus=true check-spam=true

C: enable av spam-check on email traffic

D: configure email-gateway set av-check=enabled set spam-filter=enabled

Correct Answer: D

Explanation: configure email-gateway set av-check=enabled set spam-filter=enabled properly sets up the UTM to check all email traffic for viruses and spam. This dual functionality is critical for comprehensive threat protection in email communications.

----

270. Given a scenario where a UTM device needs to provide VPN connectivity in addition to firewall protection, what is the command to configure an IPsec VPN with a pre-shared key of 'secureKey123'?

A: configure vpn type=ipsec set key="secureKey123"

B: setup vpn ipsec with key="secureKey123"

C: vpn-setup type=IPsec pre-shared-key=secureKey123 enable

D: set vpn ipsec key=secureKey123 activation

Correct Answer: C

Explanation: vpn-setup type=IPsec pre-shared-key=secureKey123 enable straightforwardly establishes a secure IPsec VPN using the specified pre-shared key, integrating network security with secure remote access capabilities, thus ensuring encrypted traffic between authenticated users and the network.

----

271. Which command configures a honeypot system to simulate a vulnerable web server on a network with IP 192.168.0.5?

A: create-honeypot 192.168.0.5 --simulate web --server

B: honeypot-setup --ip 192.168.0.5 --role web-server --status simulate

C: deploy server-honeypot 192.168.0.5 role=web simulate=true

D: setup-honeypot ip=192.168.0.5 simulate web-server vulnerable

Correct Answer: B

Explanation: The command honeypot-setup --ip 192.168.0.5 --role web-server --status simulate effectively sets up the honeypot as a web server, assigning it an IP and configuring it to simulate vulnerabilities. This makes it an ideal target for potential hackers, allowing for monitoring and analysis of attack techniques and tools without risk to actual resources.

----

272. In setting up a honeynet, what is the crucial step for ensuring it logs all incoming traffic to simulate an entire network of interactive systems?

A: honeynet-create --all-traffic --log-everything --simulate

B: honeynet-install --logging all --simulate true --network wide

C: network-honeypot --log traffic --simulate network

D: honeynet-config --capture all-traffic --mode simulate --log enable

Correct Answer: D

Explanation: honeynet-config --capture all-traffic --mode simulate --log enable ensures that the honeynet logs all incoming traffic, simulating a network environment. This setup is key for understanding network-level threats and behaviors, providing insights into large-scale attack patterns.

----

273. Fill in the blank: To deploy a honeypot that mimics a corporate email server, the essential command is _____.

A: honeypot-activate role=email --simulate mode

B: activate-honeypot --function email-server --mode simulate

C: initialize-honeypot-service --type email --mode simulation

D: set-honeypot --service email --operation simulate

Correct Answer: D

Explanation: The command set-honeypot --service email --operation simulate initiates a honeypot to emulate an email server's operations. This specific configuration is crucial for attracting and analyzing targeted email-based attacks, such as phishing or spear-phishing, which can be critical for a corporation's security assessments.

\---

274. A security technician needs to analyze the interaction between external attackers and a honeynet. Which configuration ensures that the honeynet captures detailed logs of the attacks without being exposed to real network data?

A: honeynet-setup --isolate --capture interaction --log detailed

B: deploy-honeynet security-level high --capture logs --isolate true

C: honeynet-enable --detail logging --secure isolate

D: set-honeynet-security --capture detailed --isolate network

Correct Answer: A

Explanation: With honeynet-setup --isolate --capture interaction --log detailed, the honeynet is isolated from actual data yet captures every interaction in detail. This setting allows security teams to review and analyze attacks comprehensively while ensuring that no real data is compromised during the interaction.

\---

275. Considering a scenario where a honeypot is to be integrated into an existing network, which configuration command would correctly position the honeypot to attract and analyze potential SSH brute-force attacks?

A: ssh-honeypot-setup --attract --monitor --mode active

B: honeypot-ssh --set attack=detect --config attract-mode

C: setup-ssh-honeypot --track brute-force --deploy mode=attract

D: configure-honeypot --service SSH --detection brute-force --mode attract

Explanation: configure-honeypot --service SSH --detection brute-force --mode attract perfectly positions the honeypot to detect and log SSH brute-force attempts. By setting the honeypot to attract such attacks, it provides a controlled environment to study attacker methods and strengthen defenses against one of the most common network attack vectors.

----

276. When configuring a load balancer to distribute traffic between multiple web servers, which command ensures round-robin load distribution?

A: configure-balancer method round-robin load-distribute

B: balance-load method round-robin activate distribution

C: set load-balancer algorithm round-robin enable

D: load-balancer-set method=round-robin --active

Explanation: The command set load-balancer algorithm round-robin enable ensures that the load balancer distributes incoming traffic equally among all available web servers using the round-robin method. This approach helps balance the load across servers by rotating requests in sequence, reducing the risk of server overload and improving performance.

----

277. What configuration step is essential for enabling session persistence (sticky sessions) in a load balancer for an application that requires users to maintain the same session across multiple requests?

A: set session-persistence enable timeout=300s

B: session-sticky enable with session-id for persistence

C: set session-id-persistence sticky enable timeout=150s

D: persistence-session enable with timeout=200s maintain session-id

Explanation: By using the command set session-persistence enable timeout=300s, the load balancer is configured to keep users connected to the same backend server throughout their session. This is essential for applications requiring session consistency, such as shopping carts or user authentication, to maintain smooth user experiences across multiple requests.

----

278. Fill in the blank: To ensure that the load balancer directs traffic only to healthy backend servers, the correct command to enable health checks is

_____.

A: set health-check enable for backend-servers check-interval=5s

B: enable-backend-server-healthcheck interval 10s

C: backend-health-check enable interval=7s for all servers

D: configure-health-check backend-server-health status interval=3s

Correct Answer: A

Explanation: set health-check enable for backend-servers check-interval=5s enables health checks that ensure the load balancer only routes traffic to servers that are healthy and functioning correctly. Regular health checks, at specified intervals, allow the load balancer to detect unresponsive servers and avoid sending traffic to them, which helps maintain service availability.

----

279. A company's load balancer is handling traffic for three web servers. If one server fails, the remaining servers should automatically take over the traffic. Which configuration ensures this automatic failover in the load balancer setup?

A: setup failover automatic on server failure load-balancer distribute

B: enable automatic failover load-balancer redistribute traffic failure

C: auto-failover enable load-balance distribute traffic evenly

D: configure load-balancer failover enable auto on-failure

Correct Answer: D

Explanation: The configuration configure load-balancer failover enable auto on-failure enables the load balancer to automatically redistribute traffic in the event of a server failure. This ensures uninterrupted service, as the remaining servers take over the load without manual intervention, providing a seamless failover mechanism.

----

280. In a scenario where a load balancer must prioritize HTTPS traffic over HTTP, which configuration command enables traffic prioritization while still maintaining load balancing for both protocols?

A: load-balancer traffic-distribute https priority enable http fallback

B: traffic-manager set-priority https prefer-protocol over http

C: set-priority https-traffic load-balancer fallback=http enable

D: load-balancer set traffic-priority protocol=https prefer protocol=http secondary

Correct Answer: D
Explanation: With load-balancer set traffic-priority protocol=https prefer protocol=http secondary, the load balancer is configured to prioritize HTTPS traffic, ensuring that secure traffic is handled first while still balancing traffic across both protocols. This configuration is critical for prioritizing encrypted connections, enhancing security while maintaining load balancing.

----

281. Which command in an anti-malware solution initiates a full system scan, including all files, directories, and attached drives, for malware threats?

A: scan-system malware-check full-depth include attached devices

B: full-scan initiate malware-detection deep-scan mode

C: initiate full-scan --include all --drive attach --scan-depth=maximum

D: start malware scan full system-check include external-drives

Correct Answer: C
Explanation: The command initiate full-scan --include all --drive attach --scan-depth=maximum initiates a comprehensive system-wide malware scan, including all files, directories, and connected external drives. This ensures that no potential threat is missed, even in hidden or deeply nested files.

----

282. To configure an anti-malware tool to automatically update its signature database every hour, which configuration command should be used?

A: set signature-update every-hour enable automatic refresh

B: configure update hourly-signatures enable auto

C: set update-frequency hour=1 auto-enable database-update

D: auto-update malware-signature every hour set schedule

Correct Answer: C
Explanation: The configuration set update-frequency hour=1 auto-enable database-update ensures that the anti-malware tool updates its signature database every hour automatically. Frequent updates are crucial to protect against the latest emerging threats, as malware evolves rapidly.

----

283. Fill in the blank: To enable real-time protection in an anti-malware tool, the command is _____.

A: enable real-time defense check-scan monitor all-files

B: real-time protection enable auto-scan all-files activate

C: activate real-time-protection mode=on scan-all=enabled

D: turn on real-time scanning protection enable all-scan

Correct Answer: C

Explanation: activate real-time-protection mode=on scan-all=enabled enables real-time protection in the anti-malware tool, ensuring that the system is continuously monitored for any malicious activity, with any detected threats addressed immediately as they arise.

----

284. A company's network security team wants to schedule an anti-malware scan every day at 2 AM. Which configuration ensures that the anti-malware solution runs at this specific time without impacting user activities during working hours?

A: daily-scan setup time=02:00 auto-run frequency=daily

B: set-scan-schedule time=02:00 repeat=daily frequency=24h

C: schedule scan daily at 2am set scan-parameters daily run

D: configure anti-malware scan 02:00 schedule auto-run

Correct Answer: B

Explanation: With the configuration set-scan-schedule time=02:00 repeat=daily frequency=24h, the anti-malware solution is set to scan daily at 2 AM, reducing any impact on users during working hours. Scheduling scans during off-hours ensures that system performance is not affected while maintaining consistent protection.

----

285. Considering a scenario where a known piece of malware is quarantined, which command restores the quarantined file while ensuring no malicious actions are performed on the system?

A: restore quarantined-item --scan-before-restore verify-safe

B: restore quarantined-file after-scan for safety check

C: recover quarantined malware with scan ensure file safety

D: reinstate quarantined file manual restore check for threats

Correct Answer: A

Explanation: The command restore quarantined-item --scan-before-restore verify-safe allows a quarantined file to be restored, but it ensures that the file is first scanned before it is released from quarantine. This is critical to confirm that the file no longer poses any threat to the system before it is restored to its original location.

----

286. Which command sets a firewall rule to allow only HTTPS traffic from a specific IP range (192.168.0.0/24) while blocking all other traffic?

A: allow https 192.168.0.0/24 rule firewall block others

B: configure rule allow https traffic source=192.168.0.0/24 deny-other-traffic

C: firewall-config allow-https from=192.168.0.0/24 block-rest

D: set firewall rule source=192.168.0.0/24 protocol=https action=allow block-all-others

Correct Answer: D

Explanation: The command set firewall rule source=192.168.0.0/24 protocol=https action=allow block-all-others correctly configures the firewall to permit only HTTPS traffic from the specified IP range, while all other traffic is blocked. This ensures that secure communication is allowed, while unsecure or unauthorized connections are denied access.

----

287. To configure a firewall to log all dropped packets from external sources, which configuration command should be used to enable logging?

A: set-log dropped packets from external source enable firewall

B: set firewall log dropped-packets from external sources log-enable

C: enable logging for packets drop-external action=log dropped-packets=true

D: enable drop-log for all external sources log-dropped packets

Correct Answer: C

Explanation: Using enable logging for packets drop-external action=log dropped-packets=true enables logging for all packets that are dropped from external sources. This allows administrators to monitor and audit dropped traffic, which can be crucial for identifying potential malicious activity or troubleshooting network issues.

----

288. Fill in the blank: To ensure a firewall rule prioritizes outbound traffic over inbound traffic for the HTTP protocol, the command is _____.

A: set http traffic-priority rule outbound first then inbound traffic

B: prioritize rule http outbound-over-inbound traffic enable-rule

C: prioritize http outbound first configure rule inbound later

D: configure http priority rule outbound preferred over inbound

Correct Answer: B

Explanation: The command prioritize rule http outbound-over-inbound traffic enable-rule ensures that outbound HTTP traffic is processed before inbound traffic. This is useful in scenarios where outbound traffic needs priority for bandwidth allocation or security reasons, ensuring that outgoing requests are handled before incoming responses.

----

289. A company's firewall is currently configured to allow traffic from internal servers to the internet but needs to block all incoming traffic except for SSH connections from trusted IPs. Which configuration command ensures that only SSH traffic is allowed while blocking the rest?

A: allow ssh trusted source ips firewall rule block all-incoming

B: block all except ssh allow trusted ip only firewall rule setup

C: set firewall rule allow ssh source=trusted-ips block-all-incoming

D: configure allow ssh traffic trusted-ips only block other connections

Correct Answer: C

Explanation: By using set firewall rule allow ssh source=trusted-ips block-all-incoming, the firewall is configured to allow only SSH connections from trusted IP addresses, while blocking all other incoming traffic. This enhances security by restricting access to known, trusted sources and preventing unauthorized access attempts.

----

290. Given a scenario where a firewall needs to prevent IP spoofing attacks, which command is used to implement a firewall rule that inspects source IP addresses to verify authenticity and block suspicious ones?

A: configure firewall anti-spoofing verify-source-ip enable-block-suspicious

B: firewall-config anti-spoof inspect-source-ip block-invalid-source

C: enable firewall anti-spoofing source-inspect block-ip verify

D: anti-spoof config check source-ip enable-block suspicious-ip

Correct Answer: A

Explanation: The command configure firewall anti-spoofing verify-source-ip enable-block-suspicious enables anti-spoofing protection by inspecting source IP addresses. It blocks any addresses that appear suspicious or illegitimate, providing an additional layer of security against IP spoofing attacks, where attackers attempt to disguise their source IP to gain unauthorized access.

---

291. Which command configures a proxy server to filter HTTPS traffic while allowing unrestricted HTTP traffic from all users?

A: https-filter proxy-enable allow-all-http from any user

B: filter-proxy https-enable http-allow-unrestricted all-users-access

C: proxy-config set https-filtering enable http=allow-all users

D: configure proxy filter-https allow-http all users access-allow

Correct Answer: C

Explanation: The command proxy-config set https-filtering enable http=allow-all users allows the proxy server to filter HTTPS traffic, ensuring that potentially harmful secure connections are examined, while permitting unrestricted HTTP traffic from all users. This configuration provides a balance between secure traffic management and unrestricted web access for non-secure content.

---

292. In setting up a proxy server to block access to social media sites during working hours, which command correctly applies a time-based access control policy?

A: configure time-access-control block-sites=social-media time=work-hours

B: set block social-media time-window from 9am to 5pm only

C: access-rule block social-media sites during 09:00-17:00 time-control

D: set access-control time-range=09:00-17:00 block-sites=social-media

Correct Answer: D

Explanation: set access-control time-range=09:00-17:00 block-sites=social-media correctly configures the proxy to enforce time-based access control, blocking access to social media sites during the specified working hours. This ensures employees cannot access non-work-related sites while maintaining productivity.

---

293. Fill in the blank: To enable user authentication for web traffic passing through a proxy server, the command is _____.

A: proxy-server set-authentication method=user-auth enable

B: proxy-auth enable user-authentication require auth-method=user

C: enable user-authentication proxy server set-auth type=user

D: enable proxy authentication user-check require auth-user

Correct Answer: A

Explanation: By using proxy-server set-authentication method=user-auth enable, the proxy server is set up to require user authentication before allowing web traffic through. This configuration is essential for tracking user activity and ensuring only authorized users can access the internet through the proxy.

---

294. A company wants to cache web content on its proxy server to reduce bandwidth usage for frequently accessed websites. Which configuration command enables caching for HTTP and HTTPS traffic on the proxy server?

A: enable caching http-https proxy set cache-time=1h duration

B: caching-enable for proxy http/https set cache-time=60m

C: configure caching proxy-server http+https set duration=3600s

D: enable proxy-cache protocol=http,https cache-duration=3600s

Correct Answer: D

Explanation: enable proxy-cache protocol=http,https cache-duration=3600s enables caching for both HTTP and HTTPS traffic, storing frequently accessed web content for an hour. This reduces bandwidth consumption and improves load times for users accessing the same websites repeatedly within the specified cache duration.

---

295. A proxy server is being set up to log all user activity for security auditing purposes. The company requires detailed logs of visited URLs, including timestamp, user ID, and source IP. Which command configures the proxy server to log this information?

A: logging-proxy set detail-log active include url,timestamp,user-ip

B: configure proxy-log detail-log enable include=timestamp,user-id,source-ip

C: detailed-log proxy enable urls logged include user-id,ip,time

D: proxy-server enable logging all-url log-detail with user-id,ip,timestamp

Correct Answer: B
Explanation: The command configure proxy-log detail-log enable include=timestamp,user-id,source-ip ensures that the proxy server logs detailed information, including the URLs visited by users, along with timestamps, user IDs, and the source IP address. These detailed logs are critical for auditing user activity and identifying potential security risks.

----

296. Which command sets up a risk assessment tool to identify and categorize potential cybersecurity risks across all network devices in an organization?

A: initiate risk-assessment tool network-wide scan categorize each risk

B: configure risk-assessment tool scan-all-devices categorize-risks=true

C: scan devices risk-categorization setup tool for all-network-devices

D: risk-assessment initiate scan for all devices categorize potential risks

Correct Answer: B
Explanation: The command configure risk-assessment tool scan-all-devices categorize-risks=true sets up a tool that scans all devices in the network to identify and categorize risks. This comprehensive scan allows the organization to map out all potential cybersecurity threats across its entire infrastructure.

----

297. To configure a system for automatic risk scoring based on the likelihood and impact of detected vulnerabilities, which configuration command is appropriate?

A: set risk-scoring auto-detect vulnerabilities risk-score=likelihood-impact

B: enable system for risk-score auto based on vulnerabilities detected

C: configure auto risk-score calculate by detection impact likelihood

D: risk-score setup to calculate automatically by impact likelihood score

Correct Answer: A
Explanation: By using set risk-scoring auto-detect vulnerabilities risk-score=likelihood-impact, the system automatically calculates risk scores for detected vulnerabilities based on their likelihood and impact, allowing the organization to prioritize vulnerabilities for mitigation based on their severity.

----

298. Fill in the blank: To enable continuous risk monitoring and automatically generate reports on identified risks, the correct command is _____.

A: configure continuous monitoring risk auto-report every week setup

B: enable continuous-risk-monitoring auto-reporting report-schedule=weekly

C: set automatic risk monitoring reports generated weekly system-check

D: set system for monitoring risks auto-reports generated on schedule

Correct Answer: B

Explanation: enable continuous-risk-monitoring auto-reporting report-schedule=weekly configures the system to continuously monitor risks and generate weekly reports automatically. This ensures that the organization stays informed of any new or changing risks and can act on them in a timely manner.

----

299. A company's IT team wants to implement a risk mitigation plan that automatically applies security patches when vulnerabilities are detected. Which configuration command ensures this action takes place while logging the applied patches?

A: set automatic patching vulnerability-detected log each applied patch

B: auto-patch vulnerabilities log every patch applied for audit enable

C: auto-apply patches-vulnerability-detect log-patches-applied enable

D: enable auto-patching for detected vulnerabilities log-applied patches

Correct Answer: C

Explanation: The command auto-apply patches-vulnerability-detect log-patches-applied enable ensures that whenever vulnerabilities are detected, the system automatically applies patches and logs all actions taken. This proactive approach helps mitigate risks while maintaining a record for auditing purposes.

----

300. In a scenario where an organization's risk management strategy needs to isolate critical servers from external threats automatically, which command implements this risk mitigation by adjusting firewall rules based on real-time risk detection?

A: implement firewall-adjust critical-server-isolation real-time-risk-detection

B: firewall configure auto-adjust to isolate servers based on risk alert

C: setup firewall rule adjustment for isolating servers based on risk-level

D: configure firewall to isolate critical assets when risks are detected

Explanation: implement firewall-adjust critical-server-isolation real-time-risk-detection enables real-time risk detection that automatically adjusts firewall rules to isolate critical servers from potential threats. This command ensures that high-risk servers are shielded from external attacks, helping to minimize the impact of potential security breaches.

----

301. While configuring a network for a penetration testing exercise, a cybersecurity technician sets specific rules for testing boundaries. What would be an appropriate rule to enforce the purpose and scope of ethical hacking?

A: Define clear boundaries for target systems and ensure all stakeholders agree on these limits.

B: Restricting the testing to automated scans without any manual exploitation techniques.

C: Only allowing penetration testing outside of business hours to minimize impact.

D: Limit testing to non-production systems and notify all users about potential downtime.

Correct Answer: A
Explanation: Establishing clear boundaries and obtaining agreement on these limits ensures that the penetration testing adheres to ethical standards and legal requirements, effectively mapping out the extent and limits of the testing to prevent unauthorized access to unintended targets.

----

302. A penetration tester is preparing a test environment. What command should they use on a Linux system to simulate an attack that tests network resilience?

A: sudo nmap -sP 192.168.1.0/24

B: sudo hping3 --flood --rand-source 192.168.1.100

C: tcpdump -i eth0 'port 80'

D: sudo netstat -tulpn | grep LISTEN

Correct Answer: B
Explanation: The sudo hping3 --flood --rand-source command is used to simulate a DDoS attack, which is crucial for testing the network's resilience against high volumes of traffic and random source IP addresses, thereby preparing the system against potential real-world attacks.

----

303. When documenting penetration testing procedures, which element is critical to define the scope of an ethical hack to avoid legal issues?

A: Including a detailed list of potential risks and their mitigation strategies.

B: Establishing a communication plan to be used in case of a security breach during testing.

C: Obtaining signed consent forms from all system owners and stakeholders involved.

D: Clearly outlining what systems are to be tested and what techniques are permitted.

Explanation: Defining the scope and permitted techniques in documentation is essential in ethical hacking to ensure all activities are legally compliant and authorized by all stakeholders, minimizing risks of legal repercussions and ensuring a focused testing process.

----

304. Consider a scenario where a security team is testing an application's resilience to SQL injection attacks. What would be a critical step in preparing for this penetration test?

A: Setting up a controlled environment with dummy data to monitor and analyze the behavior of the application during the attack.

B: Reviewing the application's codebase for potential vulnerabilities to tailor the attack vectors.

C: Performing a vulnerability assessment using a third-party service prior to the test.

D: Conducting preliminary scans using automated tools to identify easy exploits.

Explanation: Preparing a controlled environment with dummy data allows for safe testing of potentially destructive SQL injections, ensuring that the real data is not compromised and the impact of the attack can be fully assessed without risking operational integrity.

----

305. In an ethical hacking workshop, trainers emphasize the importance of understanding network topology before conducting a penetration test. Which command helps achieve this by mapping the network?

A: ping 192.168.1.1 -c 4

B: nmap -sn 192.168.1.0/24

C: ip route show

D: traceroute -I 192.168.1.100

Explanation: Using nmap -sn to scan the network without sending pings allows for mapping the network by silently discovering hosts without alerting the network's intrusion detection systems, providing a clear understanding of the network topology crucial for planning further penetration tests.

---

306. Which tool is used for automated vulnerability scanning and can detect a wide range of vulnerabilities across network services, databases, and web applications?

A: Nessus

B: Metasploit

C: OpenVAS

D: Qualys

Correct Answer: A

Explanation: Nessus is a comprehensive vulnerability scanner known for its broad spectrum detection capabilities that include network services, databases, and web applications, making it an indispensable tool for vulnerability assessments aiming to identify a wide array of security vulnerabilities effectively.

---

307. In a vulnerability assessment, what command is used on a Linux system to list all open ports and services to determine potential security risks?

A: sudo lsof -i -P -n | grep LISTEN

B: ps aux | grep root

C: netstat -tuln

D: ss -tulw

Correct Answer: A

Explanation: The command sudo lsof -i -P -n | grep LISTEN lists all open ports and the services that are listening on these ports, which is crucial for identifying potential security risks by revealing which services are exposed to the network.

---

308. Fill in the blank: The command ____ is used to perform an intensive scan, detect OS types, versions, and services on a network during a vulnerability assessment.

A: ping -a

B: nmap -A

C: whois domain.com

D: traceroute -I

Correct Answer: B
Explanation: The nmap -A command performs an intensive scan and is particularly valuable in vulnerability assessments for detecting operating systems, service versions, and any other services running on a network, providing a comprehensive view of potential security weaknesses.

----

309. A cybersecurity team conducts a scenario-based test to identify vulnerabilities in a web application by simulating an XSS attack. What initial step should they take using a tool?
A: Running automated scripts through Burp Suite to generate attack vectors.

B: Applying a fuzzing technique using AFL on server-side software.

C: Implementing manual SQL injection on test databases.

D: Utilizing OWASP ZAP to intercept and modify HTTP requests to the application.

Correct Answer: D
Explanation: Utilizing OWASP ZAP to intercept and modify HTTP requests provides an effective initial step in a scenario-based XSS attack simulation by enabling testers to alter inputs to the web application and observe how it handles potentially malicious scripts, thus identifying security weaknesses.

----

310. In the context of identifying system weaknesses, which technique involves passively testing security without actual exploitation of vulnerabilities?
A: Conducting a penetration test with live exploits on a cloned server environment.

B: Executing a denial-of-service attack in a controlled setting to test network resilience.

C: Performing a network sniffing session using Wireshark to observe data packets without altering them.

D: Engaging in social engineering methods to assess employee vulnerability to phishing.

Correct Answer: C
Explanation: Wireshark is used for network sniffing and is ideal for passive security testing as it allows the observation of data packets in real-time without altering the traffic, which helps in identifying vulnerable points in data transmission without impacting system integrity.

----

311. Which technique involves an attacker impersonating internal IT staff to obtain sensitive information from employees?

A: Tailgating

B: Baiting

C: Impersonation

D: Phishing

Correct Answer: C
Explanation: Impersonation as a social engineering technique is effective because attackers can exploit the trust that employees have in their IT department, thereby gaining unauthorized access to sensitive information by misleading the employees into believing they are interacting with legitimate company personnel.

----

312. When crafting a phishing email, what technical indicator should security teams monitor to identify potential threats?

A: Monitoring for unusual URL redirections in email links

B: Checking for unexpected attachments in emails

C: Observing changes in network traffic patterns

D: Analyzing the frequency of email blasts sent to employees

Correct Answer: A
Explanation: Monitoring for unusual URL redirections within email links is crucial for identifying phishing emails, as these redirections often lead to malicious sites designed to steal credentials or deploy malware, thus being a significant technical indicator for potential email-based threats.

----

313. Fill in the blank: For effective pretexting, an attacker might research an employee's _____ to fabricate a believable scenario and gain their trust.

A: work history

B: social media activities

C: recent promotions

D: personal interests

Explanation: Researching an employee's social media activities allows an attacker to gather personal information that can be used to craft believable stories or scenarios, enhancing the effectiveness of pretexting by making the false narratives more convincing and increasing the likelihood of gaining the victim's trust.

----

314. In a scenario where a cybersecurity team is testing their staff's susceptibility to phishing, what is an important first step?

A: Conducting unannounced security drills involving fake phishing attempts

B: Reviewing and updating the company's anti-phishing policies

C: Implementing stricter email filters to catch phishing attempts

D: Designing a realistic email template that mimics known contacts or organizations

Correct Answer: D
Explanation: Designing a realistic email template that closely mimics known contacts or official organizations is an important first step in conducting an internal phishing test. It ensures the test is as realistic as possible, thereby accurately gauging employees' awareness and susceptibility to actual phishing attacks.

----

315. Which social engineering technique involves gathering discarded documents from a company to gain confidential information?

A: Shoulder surfing

B: Dumpster diving

C: Eavesdropping

D: Pretexting

Correct Answer: B
Explanation: Dumpster diving is a technique used in social engineering where attackers sift through trash to find valuable information that can be pieced together to breach security. It exploits the negligence in secure disposal of confidential documents, providing attackers with access to sensitive information without direct interaction.

----

316. Which command is primarily used to discover domains and subdomains associated with a target company for initial reconnaissance?

A: traceroute example.com

B: dig +trace +noall +answer www.example.com

C: nmap -sn example.com

D: whois example.com

Correct Answer: B

Explanation: The command dig +trace +noall +answer www.example.com is used to perform a detailed query that traces the path to the domain and retrieves detailed DNS record information, making it a powerful tool for initial reconnaissance to uncover domains and subdomains linked to a target company.

----

317. What technique is most effective for identifying live hosts, open ports, and services in a target network during reconnaissance?

A: Conducting a port scan using Nmap

B: Checking for SSL/TLS certificates for web domain verification

C: Utilizing a social engineering approach to glean network info

D: Running a vulnerability assessment with Nessus

Correct Answer: A

Explanation: Using Nmap for conducting a port scan is a fundamental reconnaissance technique that allows security professionals to discover live hosts, open ports, and services, providing a map of the target network's attack surface and identifying points of vulnerability.

----

318. Fill in the blank: During reconnaissance, a security analyst uses the command ___ to query DNS records and gather information about a target organization.

A: dig -x example.com

B: ping -c 4 example.com

C: host -a example.com

D: nslookup -type=any example.com

Explanation: The command nslookup -type=any example.com queries for all types of DNS records, which can provide a wealth of information about a target organization, including server names and IP addresses, essential for detailed reconnaissance efforts.

----

319. In a simulated cyber attack scenario, what would be the first step in reconnaissance to gather intelligence on the target's email server security?

A: Conducting interviews with company IT personnel

B: Analyzing incoming and outgoing traffic patterns to the mail server

C: Examining the security features of the SMTP protocol used by the server

D: Reviewing publicly available compliance documentation on the server

Correct Answer: C
Explanation: Examining the SMTP protocol security features used by a target's email server can reveal vulnerabilities such as susceptibility to spam attacks, making it a critical first step in a scenario-based approach to understanding and evaluating the target's email security posture.

----

320. Which method is used by attackers to collect detailed information about a target's network infrastructure without sending any packets to the target network?

A: Active network scanning

B: Engaging in phishing attacks

C: Social engineering tactics

D: Passive network monitoring

Correct Answer: D
Explanation: Passive network monitoring involves observing traffic and analyzing network communications without actively engaging with the target network, allowing attackers to gather detailed information stealthily, making it a highly effective technique for collecting intelligence without detection.

----

321. What command would you use to perform a ping sweep to identify active hosts on a network segment?

A: traceroute 192.168.0.1/24

B: ping 192.168.0.1-254

C: nmap -sn 192.168.0.0/24

D: fping -a -g 192.168.0.0/24

Correct Answer: D

Explanation: The command fping -a -g 192.168.0.0/24 is designed for executing ping sweeps across a range of IP addresses, effectively identifying which hosts are active within a specified network segment. It sends a ping to each address and lists only the responsive hosts, providing a quick overview of active devices.

----

322. Which tool provides detailed analysis of network packets that can help identify devices and their roles within a network?

A: NetFlow Analyzer

B: Network Miner

C: Wireshark

D: Tcpdump

Correct Answer: C

Explanation: Wireshark is a network protocol analyzer that captures packets in real time and can dissect them to display detailed information about the network traffic. This makes it an invaluable tool for identifying devices and understanding their communication patterns and roles within a network.

----

323. Fill in the blank: To identify all live hosts in a subnet, the command _____ can be used with appropriate flags for stealth scanning.

A: nmap -sS 192.168.1.0/24

B: traceroute -I 192.168.1.1

C: ping -b 192.168.1.255

D: netstat -r

Explanation: The command nmap -sS 192.168.1.0/24 performs a SYN stealth scan, which is less intrusive and less likely to be logged by the target system's intrusion detection systems. It helps in identifying live hosts and open ports without establishing a full TCP connection, thereby providing crucial information while maintaining a lower profile.

----

324. Given the task to identify all devices connected to a corporate network and their open ports, what is the first logical step using a network scanner?

A: Conducting physical inspections of network hardware

B: Using a vulnerability scanner to detect weaknesses before scanning

C: Executing a simple SNMP walk to gather device information

D: Setting up Nmap to perform an intense scan, including service detection

Correct Answer: D
Explanation: Setting up Nmap to conduct an intense scan with service detection is the first logical step in a comprehensive network scanning procedure. This type of scan not only identifies devices and open ports but also attempts to determine the operating system and running services, giving a thorough insight into the network's architecture and vulnerabilities.

----

325. How would a cybersecurity technician use ARP scanning to effectively identify networked devices within a local area network?

A: Implementing a port mirroring session to monitor network traffic

B: Sending ARP requests to each IP on the subnet and analyzing responses

C: Using ICMP echo requests to map the network topology

D: Deploying SNMP queries across the network to identify devices

Correct Answer: B
Explanation: Using ARP scanning involves sending ARP (Address Resolution Protocol) requests to each IP address on a subnet and analyzing the ARP replies. This method effectively identifies devices on a local network by mapping IP addresses to MAC addresses, providing visibility into what devices are present on the local area network.

----

326. Which command is used on a Linux system to enumerate user accounts from the command line?

A: users

B: cat /etc/passwd

C: ls -l /home

D: whoami --all

Explanation: The command cat /etc/passwd is typically used in Unix-like operating systems to list user accounts. It allows an enumerator to view all the usernames defined on a system, which can provide a starting point for further attack strategies.

----

327. In a Windows environment, what PowerShell cmdlet can be used to list all user names available on a system network?

A: Get-NetUser

B: Get-ADUser -Filter *

C: Query-User

D: Get-WmiObject -Class Win32_UserAccount

Explanation: Get-NetUser is a PowerShell cmdlet part of the PowerView toolset that retrieves users from active directory, making it extremely effective for gathering comprehensive user account details within a Windows network environment.

----

328. Fill in the blank: To gather detailed user and machine names from a Windows domain, the command _____ can be used to query the directory services.

A: dsget user

B: net user /domain

C: ldapsearch -x

D: dsquery user

Correct Answer: D

Explanation: dsquery user is a command in Windows that queries Active Directory to retrieve user objects, which is critical for enumeration as it provides detailed information about each user, including their associated machine names if needed.

----

329. When conducting a network enumeration, what is the first step in extracting machine names from DNS using Linux command-line tools?

A: Using the host command to perform a reverse DNS lookup

B: Applying the nslookup command on known IP addresses

C: Utilizing the dig command with AXFR to request zone transfers

D: Employing the ping command to resolve hostnames

Correct Answer: A

Explanation: Using the host command to perform reverse DNS lookups can reveal machine names associated with IP addresses within the network, which is a key step in network enumeration to understand the network layout and identify potential targets.

----

330. What technique involves using SNMP to enumerate device and user information on a network?

A: Implementing a network sniff using tcpdump

B: Running a full Nmap scan with the script engine

C: Configuring SNMP walk to query public community strings

D: Executing a traceroute to monitor hop-by-hop device responses

Correct Answer: C

Explanation: Configuring SNMP walk to query public community strings is a technique that utilizes the SNMP protocol to enumerate information about network devices and user settings, which can be vital for understanding network configurations and identifying vulnerabilities.

----

331. Which command is used to exploit SQL injection in a vulnerable web application by retrieving user data?

A: sqlmap -u "http://example.com/app" --dump

B: nmap -sV --script=http-sql-injection http://example.com

C: wget --post-data="user=admin" http://example.com

D: curl -d "login=info" http://example.com/login

Correct Answer: A

Explanation: The command sqlmap -u "http://example.com/app" --dump is used for automating the process of detecting and exploiting SQL injection vulnerabilities in web applications. It efficiently extracts database information, making it an indispensable tool for penetration testers focusing on SQL injection.

----

332. What is the primary method for exploiting buffer overflow vulnerabilities in a software application?

A: Writing malicious input data that overflows the buffer and executes arbitrary code.

B: Increasing the memory allocated to application buffers to handle more data.

C: Utilizing automated scanning tools to detect buffer overflow possibilities.

D: Applying security patches to vulnerable software to test resilience.

Correct Answer: A

Explanation: Writing malicious input data that deliberately overflows the buffer and allows execution of arbitrary code is a direct method for exploiting buffer overflow vulnerabilities. This technique directly manipulates memory processes to execute attacker-controlled instructions.

----

333. Fill in the blank: The tool _____ is commonly used for automating the exploitation of known vulnerabilities in network services.

A: Nessus

B: Aircrack-ng

C: Metasploit

D: Nmap

Correct Answer: C

Explanation: Metasploit is a widely used framework for developing and executing exploit code against a remote target machine. It contains a suite of tools that help in automating the process of exploiting known vulnerabilities, making it essential for penetration testing.

----

334. In a security test, if you are trying to exploit a Cross-Site Scripting (XSS) vulnerability, what should be your initial action?

A: Creating a misleading link that directs users to a malicious site.

B: Deploying a network sniffer to capture cookies during sessions.

C: Running an automated scanner to detect XSS vulnerabilities in the application.

D: Injecting a malicious script into a web page that is reflected back to the user.

Correct Answer: D

Explanation: Injecting a malicious script into a web page that reflects the input back to the user exploits Cross-Site Scripting vulnerabilities by executing scripts in the user's browser, which can hijack user sessions, deface websites, or redirect the user to malicious sites.

----

335. What is a typical first step when using a social engineering tactic to exploit the human element of security?

A: Crafting a convincing phishing email that appears to come from a trusted source.

B: Calling the target under the pretense of IT support to ask for their password.

C: Observing and mimicking the target's behaviors to bypass security checkpoints.

D: Installing a keylogger on the target's workstation during a site visit.

Correct Answer: A

Explanation: Crafting a convincing phishing email that mimics a trusted source effectively exploits the human element of security by deceiving the recipient into disclosing confidential information or unknowingly downloading malware, highlighting the critical role of social engineering in cybersecurity breaches.

----

336. Which command correctly configures a GPU to execute a brute-force attack against an encrypted password hash using Hashcat?

A: cudaHashcat -m 400 -a 0 -o cracked.txt

B: hashcat -a 0 -m 1800 --gpu-temp-abort=85

C: cudahashcat64 -b --benchmark

D: hashcat -m 1000 -a 3 -w 4 --force

Correct Answer: D

Explanation: The chosen command uses Hashcat with the mode for NTLM hashes and a brute-force attack method, utilizing full acceleration and forcing even unsupported configurations. This setup is designed for maximum efficiency in cracking complex encrypted passwords by leveraging the GPU's full potential.

----

337. In a brute-force attack scenario, you have several strategies at your disposal. Select the approach that will likely lead to the quickest recovery of a password given modern computational capabilities.

A: Applying a brute-force attack across the full ASCII set without any restrictions or pattern assumptions.

B: Restricting the brute-force attack to alphanumeric characters only, significantly reducing the keyspace.

C: Utilizing a combination of dictionary and brute-force attacks to exploit common passwords before attempting random combinations.

D: Deploying a mask attack that tailors the brute-force process to adhere to observed password policies within the organization.

Correct Answer: C

Explanation: This option wisely combines the speed of dictionary attacks, which exploit commonly used passwords, with the thoroughness of brute-force tactics. This method effectively balances speed and coverage, making it highly effective against a wide range of common security weaknesses in password implementations.

----

338. When setting up John the Ripper to attack password hashes, what is the correct syntax to specify a wordlist and rules for a brute-force attack?

A: john --wordlist=all.txt --format=md5-gen

B: john -incremental /etc/passwd

C: john --wordlist=passwords.txt --rules --format=raw-md5

D: john --single --format=md5 /etc/shadow

Correct Answer: C

Explanation: This syntax correctly configures John the Ripper for a brute-force attack, specifying a wordlist and enabling default rules for password variations, targeting the raw MD5 hash format. It's tailored for a methodical approach in cracking hashed passwords by adapting known words through predetermined rulesets.

----

339. Given a set of potential passwords, which configuration file change in Hydra would correctly optimize a brute-force SSH login attempt?

A: Modify the task setting in Hydra to divide the password list equally among multiple instances.

B: Add '1' to the Hydra command line to utilize the maximum number of simultaneous connections, improving the brute-force attack speed.

C: Set Hydra to delay retries for 10 seconds after every 100 failed attempts to avoid triggering account lockouts.

D: Change the timeout setting in Hydra's configuration to 5 seconds, minimizing the delay between attempts.

Correct Answer: B

Explanation: This configuration adjustment optimizes the brute-force attempt by maximizing the number of simultaneous connections, which significantly enhances the speed of password cracking attempts against network services like SSH.

----

340. A cybersecurity team suspects that an intruder has gained unauthorized access using a brute-force attack. Which log file entry most likely indicates a successful brute-force password attack?

A: Multiple instances of the same user trying to login from different IP addresses within a short period.

B: Repeated access denials for user 'admin' from various unfamiliar IP addresses over a brief time.

C: User 'admin' changed their password successfully multiple times in one hour, indicating a possible security policy violation.

D: Login success for user 'admin' from IP address 192.168.1.50 at 03:15:01, after multiple failed attempts.

Correct Answer: D

Explanation: This log entry is indicative of a brute-force attack as it shows a successful login following multiple failed attempts. It's a classic pattern suggesting that the attacker tried various combinations until finding the correct password, especially when logged during unusual hours.

----

341. Identify the command that a malicious actor could use to manipulate the SUID bit and gain escalated privileges on a Linux system.

A: passwd root

B: chown root /usr/local/bin/bash

C: chmod +s /bin/bash

D: usermod -aG sudo username

Correct Answer: C

Explanation: The command chmod +s /bin/bash correctly sets the SUID bit on the bash shell, allowing any user who executes the shell to have the same privileges as the owner of the file, typically the root user. This can lead to unauthorized root access if exploited by a malicious actor.

----

342. When reviewing logs, which entry would most likely indicate an unauthorized privilege escalation attempt via a Windows scheduled task?

A: "Application Experience service entered STOPPED state unexpectedly."

B: "Task Scheduler service entered RUNNING state, task path: C:\Windows\System32\Tasks\MyTask"

C: "Service Control Manager triggered service start/stop."

D: "Windows Defender identified an unauthorized change in system settings."

Correct Answer: B

Explanation: The log entry "Task Scheduler service entered RUNNING state, task path: C:\Windows\System32\Tasks\MyTask" indicates that a specific task was initiated. If this task was configured with elevated privileges or to execute potentially harmful commands, it could be a sign of an escalation attack.

----

343. Fill in the blank: To check for privilege escalation vulnerabilities in a Linux system, the command ___ can be used to identify files with the SUID bit set.

A: lsattr /bin/bash

B: grep -R 'suid=0' /etc/passwd

C: find / -perm -4000 -exec ls -ldb {} ;

D: tail -f /var/log/auth.log

Explanation: The command find / -perm -4000 -exec ls -ldb {} \; is used to find all files across the system that have the SUID bit set, which could potentially be exploited to gain elevated privileges. Listing these files can help identify and mitigate potential vulnerabilities.

----

344. In a penetration testing scenario, what Linux command would you use to edit the /etc/sudoers file safely, aiming to add your user to the sudoers list?

A: chmod 644 /etc/sudoers

B: nano /etc/sudoers

C: EDITOR=nano visudo

D: touch /etc/sudoers

Correct Answer: C
Explanation: EDITOR=nano visudo is the correct method to safely edit the /etc/sudoers file, using nano as the editor. This approach ensures that syntax errors do not prevent sudo privileges from being correctly assigned and do not lock out administrative access.

----

345. A system administrator finds a script that exploits an application vulnerability to escalate privileges. Which entry would you expect to find in a Unix system's audit log if the script was executed?

A: System crash reported at the time 'guest' executed a high-privilege command.

B: Executed command '/bin/sh -c ./exploit_script.sh' by user 'guest'.

C: User 'admin' accessed /bin/su unexpectedly after hours.

D: Permission changed for user 'guest' from normal user to root.

Correct Answer: B
Explanation: The audit log entry "Executed command '/bin/sh -c ./exploit_script.sh' by user 'guest'" would be a clear indication that a script was executed which might have been intended to exploit vulnerabilities for privilege escalation. Monitoring such logs is critical for detecting and responding to unauthorized access attempts.

----

346. Which command line tool is typically used by attackers to establish persistence by scheduling tasks on a compromised Windows system?
A: regedit

B: net

C: at

D: schtasks

Correct Answer: D
Explanation: The schtasks command allows attackers to create, delete, configure, or display scheduled tasks on a Windows system, providing a means to execute malicious activities at predefined times or intervals, thereby ensuring persistence without manual intervention.

----

347. In a Unix environment, what file might an attacker modify to ensure their malicious script executes during system startup?
A: /bin/login

B: /etc/rc.local

C: ~/.bash_profile

D: /etc/passwd

Correct Answer: B
Explanation: Modifying /etc/rc.local allows attackers to insert commands that will execute at the end of the multi-user runlevel process during boot-up, making it a common target for ensuring a script runs every time the system starts.

----

348. Fill in the blank: To maintain access with a reverse shell, attackers often use the command ___ to listen on a compromised host.
A: set up an FTP server and connect back to a specific port.

B: employ a persistent cookie on the user's browser to reestablish connection.

C: nc -lvp 4444

D: configure a cron job to periodically connect to a specified IP address.

Correct Answer: C
Explanation: The command nc -lvp 4444 sets up a listener using netcat on port 4444, which can be used by attackers to open a backdoor for connecting back to the compromised

system. This allows maintaining access via a reverse shell that can be reconnected whenever needed.

----

349. What is the most secure method to detect unauthorized SSH key insertion used by attackers to maintain access?

A: Use intrusion detection systems (IDS) to monitor and alert on unusual SSH activities.

B: Check for frequent connections to known command and control (C&C) servers.

C: Scan for and monitor .ssh/authorized_keys files for unauthorized changes.

D: Implement network segmentation and strict firewall rules to control outgoing SSH traffic.

Correct Answer: C

Explanation: Monitoring .ssh/authorized_keys for unauthorized changes is crucial as attackers often insert their own SSH keys to gain persistent, root-level access to a compromised host. Regularly scanning and auditing this file can help detect and prevent unauthorized access.

----

350. During a security audit, you find an unknown service running on a system. Which Windows PowerShell command can you use to investigate the details and origin of the service?

A: Deploy anti-virus software to scan for known malicious signatures associated with services.

B: Check the integrity of system files using sfc /scannow to identify potential manipulations.

C: Get-Service | Where-Object {$_.DisplayName -like "unknown"} | Select-Object DisplayName, StartType, Path

D: Review installed programs through Control Panel and identify any recent installations.

Correct Answer: C

Explanation: The PowerShell command Get-Service | Where-Object {$_.DisplayName -like "*unknown*"} | Select-Object DisplayName, StartType, Path is used to identify and investigate unknown or suspicious services running on a Windows system. This command filters services by display name patterns, helping to pinpoint potentially malicious services installed during an attack.

----

351. What command can be used by attackers on a Linux system to modify the timestamp of a file to a specific date and time to hide malicious activity?

A: ls -l --time-style=full-iso

B: chmod 000 filename

C: chattr +i filename

D: touch -t 202012101830.55 filename

Correct Answer: D
Explanation: The touch -t 202012101830.55 filename command is used to change the modification and access times of the specified file to the given timestamp, thus obscuring the real time of the last modifications made by the attacker, which is crucial for hiding changes to files involved in the malicious activity.

----

352. Which of the following methods would effectively hide the presence of a malicious process from the list of running processes in a Windows environment?

A: Utilizing virtualization technology to run the malicious process entirely in a virtual machine.

B: Encrypting the process code in memory to make it difficult for security tools to scan.

C: Modifying the process image name and parent process identifier through API hooking.

D: Running the process at a lower CPU priority to avoid detection by performance monitoring tools.

Correct Answer: C
Explanation: API hooking to modify the process image name and parent process identifier can effectively make a process invisible or appear as a legitimate system process to those inspecting system process listings, thereby concealing any malicious processes.

----

353. Fill in the blank: To evade network detection mechanisms, attackers often use the command ____ to fragment packets, making it difficult for IDS to analyze them properly.

A: iptables -A OUTPUT -p tcp --tcp-flags ALL SYN,ACK -j QUEUE

B: traceroute -I target_ip

C: nc -lvp 4444 -e /bin/bash

D: hping3 --flood --rand-source target_ip

Correct Answer: A

Explanation: Using iptables -A OUTPUT -p tcp --tcp-flags ALL SYN,ACK -j QUEUE helps in fragmenting outgoing packets in a manner that makes it difficult for intrusion detection systems to reconstruct and analyze the traffic properly, aiding attackers in evading detection.

----

354. In a scenario where an attacker needs to erase their tracks on a compromised Linux system, which command should they use to securely wipe the free space of the filesystem to ensure deleted files cannot be recovered?

A: cat /dev/null > /var/log/auth.log

B: find /type f -exec rm {} +

C: shred -uzn 3 -v /dev/sda1

D: dd if=/dev/zero of=/home/user/tempfile bs=1M; rm -f /home/user/tempfile

Correct Answer: C

Explanation: The command shred -uzn 3 -v /dev/sda1 is designed to securely delete files and wipe free space by overwriting it multiple times, making recovery of deleted data extremely difficult if not impossible, which is essential for removing evidence of malicious activities on a compromised system.

----

355. During a post-attack cleanup, what Windows command might an attacker use to remove traces of executed commands from the system logs?

A: wevtutil cl System

B: attrib +h C:\Windows\Logs*

C: del %systemroot%\System32\LogFiles*

D: netsh firewall reset

Correct Answer: A

Explanation: wevtutil cl System is a Windows command used to clear the System event log, which can include logs of commands executed by an attacker. Clearing these logs is a common tactic to remove evidence of activities and hinder forensic analysis.

----

356. What is the most effective command to use in Aircrack-ng to attempt cracking a WPA2-PSK network using a pre-captured handshake file?

A: wpa_supplicant -B -c wpa_supplicant.conf -i wlan0

B: hashcat -m 2500 -a 3 handshake.hccapx -w 3

C: aircrack-ng -w wordlist.txt -b 00:11:22:33:44:55 handshake.cap

D: airdecap-ng -e ssid -p password capture-01.cap

Correct Answer: C
Explanation: The command aircrack-ng -w wordlist.txt -b 00:11:22:33:44:55 handshake.cap is effective for cracking WPA2-PSK networks as it uses a wordlist to attempt to match the pre-shared key against a previously captured handshake file, utilizing the BSSID to target the specific network.

----

357. When conducting a wireless network penetration test, which tool is primarily used to create a rogue access point to intercept wireless communications?

A: wifiphisher --essid "FreeWiFi" -aI wlan0

B: wireshark -k -i wlan0

C: airbase-ng -a 00:11:22:33:44:55 --essid "FreeWifi" -c 6

D: hostapd-wpe -c hostapd-wpe.conf

Correct Answer: C
Explanation: airbase-ng -a 00:11:22:33:44:55 --essid "FreeWifi" -c 6 is used to create a rogue access point with a specified ESSID and on a specific channel, effectively drawing users to connect to this rogue network, thereby intercepting transmitted data.

----

358. Fill in the blank: To monitor and capture wireless traffic on a specific channel, attackers use the command ____ with a compatible wireless network interface in monitor mode.

A: netsh wlan set hostednetwork mode=allow ssid=NetName key=password

B: ip link set wlan0 down; iw dev wlan0 set type monitor; ip link set wlan0 up

C: airmon-ng start wlan0 6

D: iwconfig wlan0 mode monitor; iwconfig wlan0 channel 6; tcpdump -i wlan0

Correct Answer: D
Explanation: iwconfig wlan0 mode monitor; iwconfig wlan0 channel 6; tcpdump -i wlan0 effectively sets a wireless interface to monitor mode and specifies the channel to capture packets on that channel, allowing for detailed capture of traffic for analysis or further attacks.

----

359. In an advanced Wi-Fi penetration testing scenario, which Linux command helps in deauthenticating a client from a wireless network, facilitating a man-in-the-middle attack?

A: aireplay-ng -0 2 -a 00:11:22:33:44:55 -c 11:22:33:44:55:66 mon0

B: wifite --kill -targ 00:11:22:33:44:55

C: mdk3 wlan0 d -c 6

D: iw dev wlan0 disconnect

Correct Answer: A
Explanation: aireplay-ng -0 2 -a 00:11:22:33:44:55 -c 11:22:33:44:55:66 mon0 is crucial for conducting deauthentication attacks, forcibly disconnecting the client from the network and enabling man-in-the-middle scenarios or facilitating reconnection to a rogue access point.

----

360. An attacker wants to assess the security of a wireless network encrypted with WEP. Which of the following commands would initiate the process of capturing IVs to perform a cracking attack?

A: tcpdump -i wlan0 ether host 00:11:22:33:44:55

B: airodump-ng --bssid 00:11:22:33:44:55 -c 1 --ivs -w output mon0

C: wireshark -i wlan0 -k -f "type mgt subtype beacon"

D: kismet -c wlan0

Correct Answer: B
Explanation: airodump-ng --bssid 00:11:22:33:44:55 -c 1 --ivs -w output mon0 initiates the capture of initialization vectors (IVs) from a network with WEP encryption, crucial for the subsequent cracking of the WEP key, focusing on capturing only the necessary data (IVs) for efficiency.

----

361. What command can be used to check for rooting artifacts on an Android device?

A: grep 'root' /etc/passwd

B: find / -name su

C: ls /system/app

D: cat /proc/mounts

Correct Answer: B

Explanation: The command find / -name su is straightforward and effective for searching the entire file system for the 'su' binary, which is commonly used in rooted Android devices. This helps identify unauthorized root access on the device.

----

362. When analyzing iOS app security, which tool is essential for intercepting and analyzing traffic from an iOS device to detect potential data leaks?

A: OpenSSL connected via SSH for secure communication

B: Fiddler with HTTPS decryption enabled

C: Burp Suite configured as a proxy for the device

D: Wireshark with a wireless adapter monitoring Wi-Fi traffic

Correct Answer: C

Explanation: Burp Suite configured as a proxy for the device allows for thorough inspection and manipulation of HTTP and HTTPS traffic between the iOS device and the network. This tool is instrumental in identifying and testing security vulnerabilities related to data leakage.

----

363. Fill in the blank: To view the detailed permissions of installed apps on an Android device, use the command ___.

A: dumpsys package packages

B: list packages -permissions

C: getprop ro.build.version.sdk

D: pm list packages -d

Correct Answer: D

Explanation: The command pm list packages -d (package manager) lists all packages with their detailed permission settings on an Android device, helping security professionals analyze the permissions granted to each installed application.

---

364. In a mobile penetration testing scenario, how would an attacker simulate the receipt of an SMS message on an emulated Android device to test SMS-based vulnerabilities?

A: adb shell service call isms 7 i32 0 s16 "com.android" s16 "123456" s16 "Hello"

B: adb emu sms send 123456 Hello

C: echo 'sms received 123456 Hello' | nc localhost 5554

D: sms send --port 5555 --number 123456 --text "Hello"

Correct Answer: C

Explanation: echo 'sms received 123456 Hello' | nc localhost 5554 is used to simulate an incoming SMS on an Android emulator. This command is crucial for testing how apps handle SMS inputs, which can help in discovering SMS spoofing vulnerabilities.

---

365. What command line tool is used to decrypt iOS apps, allowing for a more thorough static analysis by security professionals?

A: cycript -p <app_name>

B: otool -L <app_binary>

C: clutch -d <app_bundle_identifier>

D: gdb -x <app_script>

Correct Answer: C

Explanation: clutch -d <app_bundle_identifier> is a tool used on jailbroken iOS devices to decrypt the binary files of installed apps. Decryption is essential for performing a static analysis of the app's codebase, particularly when checking for security flaws and reverse engineering.

---

366. What AWS CLI command allows an attacker to enumerate IAM roles to potentially exploit misconfigured permissions?

A: aws s3 ls

B: aws iam list-roles

C: aws configure list

D: aws ec2 describe-instances

Correct Answer: B

Explanation: aws iam list-roles is an effective command for an attacker to list all IAM roles within an AWS environment. Identifying roles can help find potentially misconfigured or overly permissive roles that could be exploited to escalate privileges or access sensitive data.

\---

367. When scanning for vulnerabilities in Azure services, which tool can automatically detect security misconfigurations in the cloud environment?

A: Nessus

B: Azure Security Center

C: Qualys

D: Prowler

Correct Answer: D

Explanation: Prowler is a security tool designed to perform AWS security best practices assessments, auditing, hardening, and forensics readiness. It automatically checks for misconfigurations and vulnerabilities in AWS environments, making it a crucial tool for identifying security risks in Azure.

\---

368. Fill in the blank: To exploit weak container configurations in a cloud environment, an attacker might use the command ____ to execute a shell in a running Docker container.

A: docker exec -it container_id /bin/bash

B: docker run -it --rm image_name /bin/sh

C: kubectl exec pod_name -- /bin/sh

D: podman exec -it container_name /bin/sh

Correct Answer: A

Explanation: docker exec -it container_id /bin/bash is commonly used by attackers to gain interactive shell access inside a running Docker container. This command is particularly dangerous if used on containers running in production environments, as it can lead to unauthorized access and control over the containerized applications.

---

369. In cloud penetration testing, which command is used to list all the Google Cloud SQL databases in a project, potentially revealing sensitive data exposures?

A: gcloud sql instances list

B: aws rds describe-db-instances

C: azure storage account list

D: gcloud services list

Correct Answer: A

Explanation: gcloud sql instances list provides a list of all Google Cloud SQL database instances in a specified project. This information can expose sensitive data about the databases, their configurations, and operational status, potentially aiding an attacker in crafting targeted attacks.

---

370. What command line tool is primarily used for launching denial-of-service attacks against cloud-based applications to test their resilience?

A: nmap --script dos -p 80 target_ip

B: hping3 --flood target_ip

C: LOIC (Low Orbit Ion Cannon)

D: ping -t target_ip

Correct Answer: C

Explanation: LOIC (Low Orbit Ion Cannon) is a popular tool used to perform network stress testing and denial-of-service attacks. It allows attackers to test the resilience of cloud-based applications against traffic spikes and coordinated attacks, commonly used to evaluate the robustness of network infrastructures against malicious traffic volumes.

---

371. In the context of IoT security, which command would you use on a Linux-based IoT device to identify open ports that might be vulnerable to exploits?

A: sudo ifconfig

B: sudo lsof -i -P -n

C: sudo nmap -sT 192.168.1.105

D: sudo netstat -tuln

Correct Answer: C
Explanation: The command sudo nmap -sT 192.168.1.105 is used to perform a TCP connect scan, which checks for open ports on the target device. Open ports can indicate services that may be vulnerable to exploits if they are not properly secured. This command is effective for initial reconnaissance in IoT security assessments.

----

372. Which technique is essential for exploiting a known vulnerability in an IoT device's firmware when performing a penetration test?
A: Exploiting weak encryption algorithms in device communication.

B: Utilizing brute force attacks to gain administrative access.

C: Reverse engineering the firmware to inject malicious code.

D: Conducting a DDoS attack to disrupt device communication.

Correct Answer: C
Explanation: Reverse engineering the firmware allows a security professional to understand how the device operates and to identify vulnerabilities that can be exploited, such as backdoors or insecure processes. This technique is critical for crafting custom exploits tailored to the specific firmware in use.

----

373. Fill in the blank: The primary tool for intercepting and analyzing packets from an IoT device is _____.
A: ARPspoof

B: TCPdump

C: Wireshark

D: Fiddler

Correct Answer: C
Explanation: Wireshark is a network protocol analyzer that allows the capture and interactive browsing of Ethernet frames. This tool is pivotal in IoT security for analyzing the packets sent to and from devices, helping identify unencrypted transmissions and potential data leaks.

----

374. Considering an IoT device with default settings, what is a common entry point for attackers aiming to exploit these devices?

A: Sending malformed packets to overflow device buffers.

B: Use of default passwords or no passwords at all.

C: Exploiting unpatched software vulnerabilities.

D: Utilizing SQL injection on web-connected databases.

Correct Answer: B

Explanation: Many IoT devices are deployed with default credentials, which are often either easy to guess or well-documented, making them prime targets for unauthorized access. Changing default passwords is a fundamental security measure often overlooked in many IoT setups.

----

375. During a red team exercise, you identify that an IoT device is communicating over HTTP instead of HTTPS. What is the best method to exploit this vulnerability?

A: Creating a fake firmware update to install malicious software.

B: Injecting a cross-site scripting (XSS) payload into the device's web interface.

C: Using phishing emails to gain credentials from the device administrators.

D: Performing a man-in-the-middle (MITM) attack to intercept and alter the data.

Correct Answer: D

Explanation: A man-in-the-middle attack intercepts communications between two systems. If an IoT device communicates over HTTP, its data can be intercepted and potentially altered by an attacker in real-time. This method is particularly effective against devices not using encrypted communication channels like HTTPS.

----

376. What command is utilized to perform an automated scan for common vulnerabilities in a web application?

A: nikto -h www.example.com

B: nessus -x www.example.com

C: wpscan --url www.example.com

D: sqlmap -u "www.example.com/form"

Correct Answer: A

Explanation: Nikto is a powerful web server scanner that is designed to identify various types of vulnerabilities within web applications, including outdated software and potentially hazardous files or programs. This command performs a comprehensive scan against a target URL, looking for known vulnerabilities and common misconfigurations that could be exploited.

----

377. When testing for SQL injection vulnerabilities, what is a key indicator of success in an attack?

A: The application returns a database error message after input manipulation.

B: An unexpected logout occurs for the user after submitting data.

C: The login page redirects to a default error page.

D: Pages load significantly faster than when safe inputs are used.

Correct Answer: A

Explanation: The appearance of a database error message after manipulation of input suggests that the backend database might be interpreting the input as SQL code, indicating a possible SQL injection vulnerability. This means that the attacker can potentially manipulate or retrieve data directly from the database, making it a critical security flaw.

----

378. Fill in the blank: To audit the security of web session management, _____ is often used to hijack sessions.

A: Cookie tampering

B: SQL injection

C: Cross-site scripting

D: Phishing attempts

Correct Answer: A

Explanation: Cookie tampering is a technique where an attacker modifies the session cookie to escalate privileges or take over another user's session. This practice is commonly tested in security audits to check the robustness of session management and to ensure that the web application properly validates and secures session cookies.

----

379. In a scenario where a penetration tester needs to identify if a web application is vulnerable to cross-site scripting (XSS), which test input could reveal such a flaw?

A: onclick="javascript ()"

B: <iframe src="http://malicious.com"></iframe>

C: <link href="http://malicious.com/style.css" rel="stylesheet">

D: <script>alert('XSS');</script>

Correct Answer: D

Explanation: The input <script>alert('XSS');</script> is a basic but effective payload for testing cross-site scripting vulnerabilities. If this script executes and the alert box appears, it indicates that the application is not properly sanitizing user input, allowing scripts to be executed on the client side, which can lead to data theft or malicious redirection.

----

380. Describe the process a penetration tester would use to exploit a detected Local File Inclusion (LFI) vulnerability in a web application.

A: Use directory traversal sequences like ../ to escape the web root and access files.

B: Send repeated requests to the server until it crashes, revealing file paths.

C: Modify the URL parameter to include paths to sensitive files, e.g., /etc/passwd.

D: Overwrite existing files on the server to disrupt the service and test error handling.

Correct Answer: C

Explanation: Exploiting a Local File Inclusion vulnerability typically involves modifying the URL or form parameters to access or execute files on the server that should not be directly accessible. A common test is to try including system files (like /etc/passwd) to see if they can be retrieved, which would confirm the presence of an LFI flaw and potentially expose sensitive system information.

----

381. As a cybersecurity technician, you are analyzing web logs to identify potential SQL injection attempts. Which of the following log entries most likely indicates an SQL injection attack?

A: "GET /products?id=105"

B: "GET /search?q=1' DROP TABLE users; --"

C: "GET /home pageIndex=1&pageSize=20"

D: "POST /updateProfile email=user@example.com"

Explanation: This log entry contains a textbook SQL injection technique where the attacker attempts to drop a database table. Such inputs are malicious and typically aim to damage or retrieve data from the database illicitly.

----

382. In an SQL injection audit, which SQL command would be most effective for detecting vulnerable points in a web application that interacts with a database?
A: "DROP TABLE audit_log"

B: "UNION SELECT NULL, username, password FROM users WHERE 'x'='x'"

C: "EXEC sp_configure 'show advanced options', 1;"

D: "ALTER DATABASE permissions SET PUBLIC"

Explanation: The UNION SQL command is used here to test for vulnerabilities by attempting to combine the results of two selects which can reveal information about the database structure, such as table names and user details, indicating points where an attacker can inject SQL commands.

----

383. Fill in the blank: To prevent SQL injections, it is critical to use _____ to validate and sanitize user input before processing it in the SQL query.
A: "Data type constraints"

B: "Input length restrictions"

C: "Parameterized queries"

D: "Encryption at the database level"

Explanation: Parameterized queries provide a method of enforcing strict types and structures in SQL commands, which prevents attackers from altering the intent of queries by injecting malicious SQL codes.

----

384. You are tasked with designing a security training scenario for new developers. The scenario involves a web form susceptible to SQL injection. Which of the following setups would best demonstrate the vulnerability to the developers?

A: "A contact form that checks the length of the input but includes it directly in SQL commands."

B: "A login form that executes directly with inputs in a query: SELECT * FROM users WHERE username = 'input' AND password = 'input'"

C: "An order tracking page that does not show database errors to the user but fails to handle SQL errors."

D: "A feedback form that uses AJAX to post data asynchronously without proper handling."

Correct Answer: B

Explanation: This setup involves a direct insertion of user inputs into SQL queries, which does not sanitize or differentiate between code and data, thus exposing the application to SQL injections where attackers can manipulate queries to bypass authentication or retrieve data.

----

385. You are conducting a pen-test on a new web application. During the test, you manage to execute unauthorized SQL queries by manipulating user input fields. Which of the following describes the technique you most likely used?

A: "Tautology SQLi, using input such as ' or '1'='1'"

B: "Inband SQLi, extracting data using the same communication channel"

C: "Out-of-band SQLi, using DNS lookups to transmit data"

D: "Blind SQLi, relying on conditional responses to refine the payload"

Correct Answer: A

Explanation: Tautology SQLi involves inserting conditions that always evaluate to true, allowing attackers to manipulate SQL queries by extending the query logic to unauthorized purposes, such as bypassing login mechanisms or extracting data.

----

386. What type of XSS attack involves a malicious script being embedded into a web page accessed by other users?

A: "Insecure Direct Object References"

B: "DOM-based XSS"

C: "Command injection"

D: "Stored XSS"

Correct Answer: D
Explanation: Stored XSS is executed when the data provided by the attacker is saved by the server and then permanently displayed on "normal" pages returned to other users in the course of regular browsing, without proper HTML escaping.

----

387. During a security assessment, you identify a vulnerability in a web application that allows user input to include <script> tags. What type of scripting vulnerability does this represent?
A: "Cross-site request forgery"

B: "Server-side request forgery"

C: "Local file inclusion"

D: "Reflected XSS"

Correct Answer: D
Explanation: Reflected XSS occurs when user input is immediately returned by web applications without proper validation and escaping, allowing an attacker to craft a URL that includes malicious JavaScript code which is executed when the URL is visited.

----

388. Fill in the blank: To mitigate XSS vulnerabilities, it is essential to implement _____ on all user-submitted data.
A: "Token-based authentication"

B: "Input sanitization"

C: "Using HTTPS exclusively"

D: "Database encryption"

Correct Answer: B
Explanation: Input sanitization is critical as it removes or escapes special characters from the user input that could potentially be used to inject malicious scripts, thereby preventing XSS attacks.

----

389. You are tasked with constructing a security scenario to demonstrate an XSS attack through a user profile page that allows users to enter descriptions. What scenario best illustrates an XSS attack?

A: "Creating a fake login form that sends credentials to an attacker's server"

B: "Injecting a script that redirects users to malicious sites through clickable links"

C: "Embedding a malicious script in the user's profile description that executes when viewed by others"

D: "Sending a URL with a malicious script to the admin through the contact form"

Correct Answer: C
Explanation: Embedding malicious scripts in profile descriptions that execute upon viewing by others showcases a classic stored XSS scenario, demonstrating how persistent scripts can provide ongoing access to users' browsers.

----

390. As part of a penetration testing team, you're demonstrating an XSS attack on a live chat feature of a website. Which XSS payload would you use to alert all users to the vulnerability?

A: "<script>alert('XSS detected!');</script>"

B: "<iframe src='http://malicious.com'></iframe>"

C: "<script>document.write('You are hacked');</script>"

D: "<img src='javascript:alert(\"XSS!\");'>"

Correct Answer: A
Explanation: Using a simple alert script in an XSS payload is an effective demonstration of the vulnerability. It shows how attackers can execute JavaScript code in the context of the user's session, alerting users to the presence of the security flaw.

----

391. What is the primary objective of a buffer overflow attack in cybersecurity?
A: "Executing arbitrary code on the target system"

B: "Disrupting service to create a denial of service (DoS) condition"

C: "Stealing confidential data directly from the memory"

D: "Corrupting data to cause application errors"

Correct Answer: A

Explanation: Buffer overflow attacks aim to exploit memory handling bugs in software to execute arbitrary code. By overwriting memory segments, such as the return pointer in a call stack, attackers can divert the execution path to malicious payloads.

----

392. Which programming language is most susceptible to buffer overflow vulnerabilities due to its lack of intrinsic safety checks?

A: "Java"

B: "JavaScript"

C: "C and C++"

D: "Ruby"

Correct Answer: C

Explanation: C and C++ are notorious for their susceptibility to buffer overflow vulnerabilities as they do not enforce bounds checking automatically, making it easy for programmers to overlook safe memory management.

----

393. Fill in the blank: To protect against buffer overflow attacks, it is crucial to implement _____ checks on all inputs.

A: "Type"

B: "Semantic"

C: "Syntax"

D: "Boundary"

Correct Answer: D

Explanation: Implementing boundary checks on all inputs ensures that the size of the input does not exceed the allocated memory, thus preventing attackers from overwriting adjacent memory and potentially controlling the application.

----

394. During a code audit of a C++ application, you discover a function that handles user input without limits. What should you suggest to mitigate the risk of a buffer overflow?

A: "Integrate automated bounds checking for array inputs"

B: "Rewrite the application to handle exceptions properly"

C: "Use a more modern programming language like Python"

D: "Encourage the use of strong user authentication methods"

Correct Answer: A
Explanation: Integrating automated bounds checking, particularly in languages like C++, helps in safely managing arrays and pointers, directly addressing the common cause of buffer overflows by preventing out-of-bounds memory access.

----

395. You are tasked with demonstrating a buffer overflow attack on an application that uses unsafe string operations. Which method would be most effective?
A: "Utilizing SQL injection to bypass input validation"

B: "Sending repeated requests to exhaust server memory"

C: "Crafting inputs that overwrite the return address on the stack"

D: "Manipulating user session IDs to hijack user sessions"

Correct Answer: C
Explanation: Overwriting the return address on the stack with crafted inputs allows an attacker to control the execution flow of the program, demonstrating a classic stack-based buffer overflow attack. This technique involves inserting a new return address pointing to attacker-controlled code.

----

396. In a CTF competition, which tool is best suited for conducting a network sniffing challenge to capture and analyze traffic?
A: "Nmap"

B: "Metasploit"

C: "Wireshark"

D: "Burp Suite"

Correct Answer: C
Explanation: Wireshark is a network protocol analyzer that allows users to capture and interactively browse the traffic running on a computer network, making it ideal for network sniffing challenges in a CTF context to analyze and understand traffic patterns or intercept communications.

----

397. What type of CTF challenge involves participants exploiting a vulnerable web application to retrieve hidden data from a server?

A: "Network attack"

B: "Binary exploitation"

C: "Web exploitation"

D: "Forensic challenge"

Correct Answer: C
Explanation: Web exploitation challenges typically involve identifying and exploiting security flaws in web applications, such as SQL injection, XSS, or file inclusion vulnerabilities, to retrieve hidden data or flags on the server, demonstrating practical attack vectors on web-based interfaces.

----

398. Fill in the blank: During a CTF event, _____ tools are often used to decode or decrypt cryptographic challenges.

A: "Packet crafting"

B: "Hash cracking"

C: "Brute force attack"

D: "Cryptanalysis"

Correct Answer: D
Explanation: Cryptanalysis tools are essential in CTFs for decoding or decrypting encrypted messages or data that are part of cryptographic challenges, helping participants understand encryption mechanisms and how they can be broken or circumvented.

----

399. You are participating in a CTF challenge that requires identifying and exploiting an SQL injection vulnerability in a web application. What would be the most effective first step?

A: "Using a vulnerability scanner on the server hosting the application"

B: "Creating a denial of service attack to disrupt the application"

C: "Testing input fields for typical SQL injection payloads"

D: "Reviewing the source code of the application for vulnerabilities"

Correct Answer: C

Explanation: Testing input fields for typical SQL injection payloads as the first step in exploiting vulnerabilities allows participants to quickly identify insecure handling of user input, which can lead to unauthorized data access or manipulation in a web application.

----

400. In a reverse engineering CTF challenge, you are given a binary file to analyze. Which technique is most commonly used to understand its functionality?

A: "Disassembling the binary to view the assembly code"

B: "Running the binary in a sandbox environment to observe behavior"

C: "Monitoring network traffic generated by the binary"

D: "Checking the binary for strings of interest like URLs or credentials"

Correct Answer: A

Explanation: Disassembling the binary to view its assembly code is a common approach in reverse engineering tasks, as it allows the analyst to directly interpret the low-level instructions that govern the program's behavior, providing insights into its functionality and potential vulnerabilities.

----

401. When initiating the containment phase in an incident response, which command effectively isolates a compromised system within a Linux environment without disrupting network evidence?

A: sudo ifconfig eth0 down

B: sudo iptables -I INPUT 1 -s 192.168.1.105 -j DROP

C: sudo route add 192.168.1.105 reject

D: sudo ufw deny from 192.168.1.105

Correct Answer: B
Explanation: Using sudo iptables -I INPUT 1 -s 192.168.1.105 -j DROP quickly blocks incoming traffic from the suspected IP address without disrupting outgoing traffic, allowing for ongoing examination of the system while preventing further compromise.

----

402. During the identification phase of a cybersecurity incident, what command would you use to view all current connections and listening ports on a system to determine potential unauthorized access?

A: sudo netstat -tulnp

B: sudo ss -tuln

C: sudo lsof -i

D: sudo who -a

Correct Answer: A
Explanation: The command sudo netstat -tulnp provides detailed information about all active connections and listening ports, including the PID and program names, which are crucial for identifying unauthorized or suspicious activities during the identification phase.

----

403. In the preparation phase of incident response, what is the primary configuration file for setting up logging on a Linux system to ensure all actions are recorded for later analysis?

A: /etc/syslog.conf

B: /etc/security/limits.conf

C: /etc/rsyslog.conf

D: /etc/logrotate.conf

Explanation: /etc/rsyslog.conf is pivotal for configuring system logging in Linux. Proper configuration ensures that all system and service logs are captured, which is fundamental for forensic analysis if an incident occurs.

----

404. After detecting an anomaly that could indicate a breach, which of the following steps should be taken first in the analysis phase of incident response?

A: Quarantine the affected systems and apply the latest security patches.

B: Conduct a meeting with the incident response team to discuss the breach.

C: Perform a comprehensive system scan to identify the source and method of the breach.

D: Notify law enforcement and regulatory bodies immediately.

Explanation: Performing a comprehensive system scan as the initial step in the analysis phase ensures that the full scope of the breach is understood, helping to identify the intrusion's source and the methods used by the attackers.

----

405. A security analyst suspects that an incident is a part of a larger campaign. What initial action should the analyst take during the recovery phase to prevent future occurrences?

A: Implement additional monitoring tools across the network.

B: Analyze related incidents to identify patterns or common indicators of compromise.

C: Restore all systems from the most recent clean backup.

D: Update firewall and intrusion detection system rules to enhance defenses.

Explanation: Analyzing related incidents to identify patterns or common indicators of compromise during the recovery phase can significantly aid in understanding the attack vectors and strengthening the system against similar future incidents.

----

406. What command is used to create a bit-for-bit disk image for forensic analysis in Linux?

A: rsync -avh /dev/sda /path/to/output.img

B: dd if=/dev/sda of=/path/to/output.img bs=4096 conv=noerror,sync

C: cp /dev/sda /path/to/output.img

D: tar -czvf backup.tar.gz /dev/sda

Correct Answer: B
Explanation: Using dd if=/dev/sda of=/path/to/output.img bs=4096 conv=noerror,sync ensures a thorough and accurate disk image is created, capturing all data byte-for-byte, including recoverable deleted files, which is essential for forensics.

---

407. In the context of digital forensics, which file system is known for its detailed logging of file system transactions, useful in timeline analysis?
A: ReiserFS, known for its journaling capabilities that help in recovering corrupted data.

B: HFS+, used in older macOS environments, which logs detailed metadata for files.

C: NTFS due to its Master File Table (MFT) that records every file transaction.

D: Ext4, as it is commonly used in Linux environments and supports file versioning.

Correct Answer: C
Explanation: NTFS is preferred in digital forensics for its Master File Table (MFT) that meticulously records details about every file transaction, making it invaluable for constructing a timeline of events.

---

408. Which tool is essential for analyzing memory dumps to find traces of malware activity during a digital forensics investigation?
A: Volatility, as it supports numerous plugins for analyzing process and kernel memories.

B: EnCase, a comprehensive tool for forensic analysis across different platforms.

C: Autopsy, which provides a graphical interface for managing forensic investigations.

D: FTK Imager, known for its ability to create and analyze disk images quickly.

Correct Answer: A
Explanation: Volatility is a powerful tool in forensic investigations for analyzing volatile memory (RAM) dumps to detect and analyze malware, which can often be found residing in memory during attacks.

---

409. When tasked with recovering deleted emails for a case, what is the first step a forensic investigator should take upon receiving the hard drive?

A: Immediately start searching for emails to assess the volume of deleted content.

B: Conduct a preliminary scan of the hard drive to assess the amount of recoverable data.

C: Analyze the file system to determine which email client was used by the suspect.

D: Create an exact clone of the hard drive to avoid data corruption and ensure all data is preserved.

Correct Answer: D
Explanation: The initial step of cloning the hard drive ensures that all data is preserved in its original state, which is crucial for forensic integrity and admissibility in court.

----

410. A forensic expert needs to present evidence from logs that indicate the time of unauthorized access. What format should the timestamps be converted to for clarity and legal acceptance?

A: Unix time format, as it represents the number of seconds past since January 1, 1970.

B: RFC 2822 format, commonly used in email headers and understood in legal proceedings.

C: Localized string format, adjusted for the legal jurisdiction of the investigation.

D: ISO 8601 standard format for timestamps to ensure they are clear and universally understood.

Correct Answer: D
Explanation: Converting timestamps to the ISO 8601 standard ensures that they are precise, easy to understand, and accepted in legal contexts worldwide, which aids in establishing a clear timeline of events.

----

411. What is the first step in establishing a digital chain of custody for a hard drive containing sensitive data?

A: Photograph the hard drive and its connections before removal from a computer.

B: Create a detailed evidence log entry as soon as the hard drive is received, documenting its receipt.

C: Seal the hard drive in a forensic bag without any additional documentation.

D: Immediately duplicate the hard drive using a write-blocker device.

Explanation: Creating a detailed log entry immediately upon receipt of a hard drive establishes a clear initial point in the chain of custody, ensuring all subsequent handlers and procedures are meticulously recorded.

----

412. Which cryptographic method is most recommended for ensuring the integrity of digital evidence files?

A: Generate SHA-256 hashes for files and store them securely with the evidence.

B: Employ digital signatures and timestamps for each file accessed.

C: Use MD5 hashing algorithm for quicker processing of large files.

D: Implement AES encryption on all digital evidence files.

Correct Answer: A
Explanation: Generating SHA-256 hashes provides a highly reliable means of verifying the integrity of evidence files, as SHA-256 is resistant to hash collisions, making it a staple in forensic procedures.

----

413. Fill in the blank: The form used to record the transfer of evidence and all individuals who handled it is called a _____.

A: Transfer sheet.

B: Chain form.

C: Custody log.

D: Evidence record.

Correct Answer: C
Explanation: The "Custody log" is essential for maintaining a clear record of all personnel who have handled the evidence, documenting each transfer and maintaining continuity of custody.

----

414. When transferring evidence from a crime scene to the lab, what is the best practice for packaging digital media like CDs and USB drives?

A: Use anti-static bags to prevent electrostatic damage and label each with a tamper-evident seal.

B: Place digital media in padded envelopes and mark them with the case number.

C: Wrap digital media in bubble wrap and place it in a cardboard box.

D: Store digital media in any available container without specific labeling.

Correct Answer: A
Explanation: Using anti-static bags and tamper-evident seals not only protects digital media from physical and electrostatic damage but also visibly indicates if the evidence has been accessed or tampered with.

----

415. In a legal case, how should an investigator document the process of acquiring digital evidence to ensure admissibility?

A: Maintain a mental note of actions taken for later recounting in reports.

B: Prepare a verbal summary to be presented during initial evidence review.

C: Log all actions in an online database without timestamps or signatures.

D: Write a detailed report that includes every action taken with the evidence, time-stamped and signed.

Correct Answer: D
Explanation: Writing a detailed report with timestamps and signatures for every interaction with evidence ensures a comprehensive, auditable document that can be used to verify the integrity and continuity of evidence in legal proceedings.

----

416. What command is used to create a forensic image of a USB drive /dev/sdb in Linux?

A: dd if=/dev/sdb of=/path/to/image.img bs=512 conv=noerror,sync

B: tar -zcvf /dev/sdb /path/to/archive.tar.gz

C: cp /dev/sdb /path/to/backup.img

D: rsync -avh /dev/sdb /path/to/sync_folder/

Correct Answer: A
Explanation: Using dd if=/dev/sdb of=/path/to/image.img bs=512 conv=noerror,sync ensures a sector-by-sector copy of the USB drive, capturing all data exactly as it is, including deleted or hidden files, which is crucial for maintaining the integrity of forensic evidence.

----

417. Which software is preferred for remote data acquisition from a Windows workstation across a network?

A: Axiom Cyber

B: Wireshark

C: FTK Remote Agent

D: EnCase Forensic Imager

Correct Answer: D
Explanation: EnCase Forensic Imager allows for secure and reliable remote data acquisition, making it a suitable choice for accessing data on a Windows workstation across a network, providing comprehensive logging and integrity verification.

----

418. Fill in the blank: The primary tool used for volatile data acquisition in memory forensics is _____.

A: Redline

B: FTK Imager

C: MemDump

D: Volatility

Correct Answer: B
Explanation: FTK Imager is a widely recognized tool for acquiring volatile data, especially useful in memory forensics for capturing live system memory accurately and efficiently, which can then be analyzed for evidence of running processes, network connections, and more.

----

419. When acquiring data from a smartphone, what is the first step to ensure data integrity and prevent data modification?

A: Install a mobile device management (MDM) solution to oversee the device.

B: Encrypt the device storage to secure data before acquisition.

C: Enable airplane mode on the device to disable wireless signals.

D: Physically disconnect the device from any network connections to prevent remote wipes or updates.

Correct Answer: D
Explanation: Physically disconnecting a smartphone from network connections immediately upon acquisition is critical to prevent any remote commands that could alter or wipe the data, thus preserving the original state of digital evidence.

----

420. A forensic investigator needs to acquire data from a damaged hard drive suspected to contain critical evidence. What is the best approach?

A: Use a hardware write-blocker before attempting to clone the drive to ensure no data is written during the process.

B: Connect the drive to a Linux system and use ddrescue to clone it.

C: Freeze the drive to attempt recovery of data by dealing with stuck components.

D: Attempt to boot the system normally and back up files through the operating system.

Correct Answer: A
Explanation: Employing a hardware write-blocker when dealing with a damaged hard drive is essential to prevent any accidental writes during the data acquisition process, ensuring that the evidence remains unaltered and forensically sound for subsequent analysis.

----

421. What command in Linux would you use to create a bit-by-bit image of a hard drive located at /dev/sda and output the image to /mnt/forensics/drive.img?

A: rsync -av /dev/sda /mnt/forensics/drive.img

B: tar -czf /mnt/forensics/drive.img /dev/sda

C: dd if=/dev/sda of=/mnt/forensics/drive.img bs=4096 conv=noerror,sync

D: cp /dev/sda /mnt/forensics/drive.img

Correct Answer: C
Explanation: Using dd if=/dev/sda of=/mnt/forensics/drive.img bs=4096 conv=noerror,sync creates a perfect bit-by-bit image of the hard drive, capturing all sectors, including those that are empty or contain deleted data. The conv=noerror,sync options ensure that errors are logged but skipped, preserving as much data as possible.

----

422. Which tool is best suited for creating forensic images of digital storage while ensuring the integrity of the data using a write-blocker?

A: Volatility with an external write-blocker for forensic acquisition of hard drives.

B: dd with a built-in write-blocker configuration to ensure no changes to the original drive.

C: EnCase Forensic Imager combined with a hardware write-blocker for complete data integrity.

D: FTK Imager with a software write-blocker enabled to prevent data corruption.

Correct Answer: C
Explanation: EnCase Forensic Imager, combined with a hardware write-blocker, ensures that no data is written back to the original drive during imaging, preserving the integrity of the evidence while providing detailed logs for forensic analysis.

----

423. Fill in the blank: The most critical aspect of creating a forensic image is to ensure that no _____ is written back to the original storage device during the imaging process.

A: Timestamp.

B: Metadata.

C: Data.

D: Hash.

Correct Answer: C
Explanation: Ensuring that no data is written to the original device is critical when creating forensic images because any changes can alter the evidence and compromise its admissibility in court.

----

424. You are tasked with creating a forensic image of a damaged hard drive that may have bad sectors. What method would ensure that the imaging process skips bad sectors while still preserving the rest of the data?

A: Implement a file backup tool that selectively copies only accessible data, avoiding corrupt areas.

B: Use the ddrescue command, which is designed for imaging drives with bad sectors, ensuring data is not lost.

C: Use the rsync command to copy the data while skipping any corrupt sectors.

D: Leverage file carving tools to recover only the usable files from the drive and discard the rest.

Correct Answer: B

Explanation: The ddrescue command is specifically designed for imaging faulty or damaged drives. It attempts to read data from bad sectors multiple times, and if it fails, it skips them, allowing recovery of the rest of the data without compromising the integrity of the image.

----

425. A forensic investigator needs to create a forensic image of a network storage device over the network using a tool that supports multiple file formats. Which tool should the investigator use to perform this task?

A: Sleuth Kit with built-in acquisition capabilities but requires manual setup for imaging over the network.

B: Autopsy, which supports network acquisition for forensic imaging but is limited in file format options.

C: FTK Imager for its ability to work over networks and support various file formats like E01, RAW, and AFF.

D: Axiom Cyber, which allows remote imaging and analysis but has limited support for file formats.

Correct Answer: C

Explanation: FTK Imager is an excellent tool for imaging network storage devices, as it supports remote acquisition and multiple forensic image formats, such as E01, RAW, and AFF, allowing investigators to choose the best format for their needs while maintaining data integrity.

----

426. Which command in Volatility is used to list all processes running in memory to identify potential malicious processes?

A: volatility -f memory.dmp --profile=Win7SP1x64 pstree

B: volatility -f memory.dmp --profile=Win7SP1x64 pslist

C: volatility -f memory.dmp --profile=Win7SP1x64 procdump

D: volatility -f memory.dmp --profile=Win7SP1x64 psxview

Explanation: The volatility -f memory.dmp --profile=Win7SP1x64 pslist command provides a detailed listing of all processes running in memory. This is crucial for detecting processes that are either malicious or unexpected in the memory of a compromised system.

----

427. When analyzing memory dumps for signs of malware, which tool is most effective for detecting injected processes that do not show up in normal process listings?

A: Axiom Cyber, which can search for malicious memory alterations.

B: EnCase Forensic Imager, which can highlight abnormal processes in the memory dump.

C: Volatility's malfind plugin, which detects injected code in processes and flags suspicious memory segments.

D: FTK Imager, which supports scanning for hidden or injected processes in memory dumps.

Explanation: The malfind plugin in Volatility is highly effective in identifying malicious code injected into processes that might not appear suspicious at first glance. It scans for suspicious memory regions and injected code that normal process listing commands may miss.

----

428. Fill in the blank: A forensic investigator needs to extract the registry hives from a memory dump to analyze potential persistence mechanisms. The command they would use in Volatility is _____.

A: registrystats

B: dumpregistry

C: hivelist

D: volshell

Explanation: The hivelist command in Volatility allows investigators to extract the registry hives from a memory dump. These hives can be analyzed for persistence mechanisms like autostart entries, malware configurations, and system settings.

----

429. You are tasked with analyzing memory from a compromised Windows system. After running a process listing, you notice several processes with suspicious command-line arguments. What is the best next step to confirm if any processes were injected with malicious code?

A: Use the malfind command to search for hidden or injected malicious code in processes.

B: Investigate the handles associated with the processes using the handles command.

C: Scan the memory for anomalous network connections tied to the suspicious processes using the netscan command.

D: Dump the memory contents of the processes using procdump and analyze them for malicious content.

Correct Answer: A
Explanation: The malfind command is essential for investigating potentially malicious processes that show unusual behavior. By examining these processes, investigators can detect injected code or rootkits that alter the legitimate processes.

----

430. During memory analysis, a forensic investigator discovers a process that is not listed in the standard Windows task manager but is visible in the memory dump. What technique can be used to gather more information about this hidden process?

A: Review process creation logs in event viewer to confirm if the process was legitimate.

B: Investigate kernel objects associated with the process using the kdbgscan command to see if it interacts with the kernel.

C: Use the ldrmodules command to identify discrepancies in loaded modules, which often reveal hidden or injected processes.

D: Look at open files tied to the process using the filescan command to determine if it has accessed critical system files.

Correct Answer: C
Explanation: The ldrmodules command helps reveal discrepancies between the loaded modules reported by a process and those actually loaded in memory. This discrepancy often indicates the presence of hidden or malicious code injected into the system, which can evade standard detection mechanisms.

----

431. What command is used to create a forensic disk image of a hard drive located at /dev/sda while skipping bad sectors and logging errors?

A: dd if=/dev/sda of=/mnt/forensics/image.img conv=sync,noerror

B: cp /dev/sda /mnt/forensics/image.img

C: tar -cf /mnt/forensics/image.tar /dev/sda

D: ddrescue /dev/sda /mnt/forensics/image.img /mnt/forensics/image.log

Correct Answer: D

Explanation: The ddrescue /dev/sda /mnt/forensics/image.img /mnt/forensics/image.log command is specifically designed to create a forensic image of a disk while safely skipping bad sectors. It logs any errors encountered, ensuring the rest of the data is captured correctly for analysis.

----

432. Which tool allows a forensic investigator to view the Master File Table (MFT) on an NTFS partition to identify deleted files and timestamps?

A: Sleuth Kit, a suite of tools that includes functionality for reading the MFT on NTFS file systems.

B: Axiom Cyber, which enables investigators to export and analyze the MFT in various forensic formats.

C: FTK Imager, which allows the investigator to read and analyze the Master File Table (MFT) on NTFS partitions.

D: EnCase, which includes a feature for analyzing the MFT on NTFS volumes for evidence of deleted or modified files.

Correct Answer: C

Explanation: FTK Imager is a widely recognized tool in forensic investigations that allows examiners to access the Master File Table (MFT) of an NTFS partition. This provides valuable insights into deleted files and the time when they were last accessed or modified.

----

433. Fill in the blank: The process of verifying the integrity of a forensic image is typically done by generating a _____ hash of both the original disk and the image file.

A: CRC32

B: SHA-256

C: MD5

D: HMAC

Explanation: Using a SHA-256 hash ensures a high level of integrity checking when verifying the forensic image against the original disk. This hash is commonly used because of its collision resistance and reliability in forensic workflows.

----

434. You are tasked with examining a hard drive suspected of containing malware. Upon inspecting the drive, you notice hidden partitions. What is the best command to list all partitions, including hidden ones, for further analysis?
A: blkid

B: lsblk

C: fdisk -l

D: parted -l

Explanation: The fdisk -l command is a standard tool for listing all partitions, including hidden or unmounted ones. This is critical when investigating hidden partitions that attackers may use to store malicious or unauthorized data.

----

435. During a disk forensic investigation, an investigator needs to identify files that have been recently accessed or modified. What method should be used to determine the last access times of files on an NTFS volume?
A: Analyze the timestamps recorded in the $Standard_Information attribute for each file in the MFT.

B: Utilize file carving techniques to recover files and infer their last access time based on metadata.

C: Use volume shadow copies to compare historical file states and determine file access times.

D: Use the $LogFile and $MFT from the NTFS volume to check file system activity, including file access times and modifications.

Correct Answer: D

Explanation: Analyzing the $LogFile and $MFT on an NTFS volume allows investigators to track file system activity, including when files were last accessed or modified. These records are essential for establishing timelines and identifying suspicious activity.

----

436. What is the most appropriate tool for real-time packet capture and analysis that allows you to implement complex filters to detect potential intrusions?

A: Nmap is primarily used for network scanning and security auditing but does not support real-time analysis or complex filtering required for intrusion detection.

B: Wireshark uses powerful filtering capabilities to selectively examine the packet data passing through the network, making it an ideal choice for detailed traffic analysis.

C: Fiddler captures HTTP and HTTPS traffic data but is not adequate for comprehensive network traffic analysis in a security context.

D: Tcpdump, though useful, lacks the real-time analysis and deep packet inspection capabilities of more sophisticated tools.

Correct Answer: B

Explanation: Wireshark is highly effective for real-time traffic analysis due to its extensive filtering options and ability to decode different protocols, which makes it indispensable for detecting and analyzing network intrusions as they occur.

----

437. In the context of identifying unauthorized data exfiltration, what configuration would you implement on an IDS to monitor large outbound transfers that deviate from normal network behavior?

A: Deploy anomaly-based detection in the IDS to automatically adapt to changing network behaviors without predefined thresholds.

B: Use the IDS to only log traffic for manual review at regular intervals, focusing on peak usage hours to reduce data volume.

C: Configure the IDS rules to alert when the daily threshold of outbound traffic exceeds 3 GB from a single device, as it may indicate data leakage.

D: Set a low sensitivity on IDS to avoid unnecessary alerts, focusing on detecting malware signatures rather than traffic volumes.

Correct Answer: C

Explanation: By setting an alert for abnormal outbound traffic volumes, this configuration helps in early detection of potential data exfiltration attempts, which is crucial for preventing data breaches.

----

438. Fill in the blank: To analyze historical network traffic for intrusion evidence, the command line utility _____ is used for parsing pcap files to reconstruct TCP/IP sessions.

A: ngrep

B: tcpflow

C: snort

D: wireshark

Correct Answer: B

Explanation: Tcpflow is specifically designed for parsing pcap files and reconstructing the data streams, making it useful for detailed post-event analysis of network intrusions.

----

439. During a simulated attack, you notice an anomaly in DNS requests. What type of analysis should be conducted to track the source of potentially malicious activity?

A: Perform a statistical analysis of DNS query volumes and timing to detect unusual patterns that may suggest domain generation algorithms (DGA) used by malware.

B: Utilize a behavioral heuristics approach to evaluate the legitimacy of each DNS request based on past trends and known benign sources.

C: Apply machine learning algorithms to classify DNS traffic as normal or suspicious based on continuous learning from network traffic patterns.

D: Conduct a root cause analysis using historical log data to identify the origin of the DNS anomalies and assess potential impacts.

Correct Answer: A

Explanation: Statistical analysis of DNS queries can help identify patterns that deviate from the norm, which might be indicative of malware communication with command-and-control servers using DGA.

----

440. After discovering suspicious network traffic originating from a set of internal IP addresses, which approach would best facilitate the identification and tracking of the responsible devices?

A: Implement strict ACLs that restrict access based on the minimum necessary principle, reducing the risk of internal traffic becoming malicious.

B: Set up a network segmentation strategy that isolates the suspicious IPs and closely monitor all ingress and egress traffic with dedicated log analysis.

C: Employ a SIEM system to correlate data from various sources for a holistic view of network security but not specifically to track individual devices.

D: Increase the encryption level across the network to prevent data from being readable by unauthorized parties.

Correct Answer: B

Explanation: Network segmentation provides an effective way to control suspicious traffic by isolating it for more detailed scrutiny and preventing potential threats from spreading across the network.

----

441. What software tool is best suited for bypassing lock screens on Android devices to access data for forensic analysis?

A: UFED provides capabilities to unlock and extract data from various smartphone models without altering the device data, preserving its forensic integrity.

B: ADB can be used to access Android devices, but it requires USB debugging to be enabled, which might not be feasible in a forensic situation.

C: Fastboot mode allows for bypassing certain security features on Android devices, but it does not provide comprehensive data access for locked devices.

D: Odin is specific to Samsung devices for firmware flashing and does not generally support bypassing the lock screen for forensic analysis.

Correct Answer: A

Explanation: UFED is renowned in the mobile forensics community for its extensive support for various devices and its ability to bypass security mechanisms without compromising the integrity of the data, which is critical for legal proceedings.

----

442. In a scenario where you need to recover deleted text messages from an iPhone, which filesystem should you focus on during your forensic examination?

A: Target the HFS+ filesystem, which was used in older iOS versions and may not hold current data from the latest iOS devices.

B: Examine the Ext4 filesystem used in older Android devices, which may contain residual data but is not relevant for iPhones.

C: Focus on examining the AFPS filesystem, as it is used by modern iPhones and contains all user data, including deleted messages.

D: Investigate the YAFFS2 filesystem commonly found in older Android models, which has no relevance to iPhone data recovery.

Correct Answer: C
Explanation: The AFPS filesystem is crucial in modern iPhones for forensic analysts because it handles all user data storage, including areas where deleted data may reside, making it the primary target for recovery of such data.

----

443. Fill in the blank: _____ is a popular tool for creating a physical image of an iOS device, crucial for comprehensive forensic investigations.

A: Cellebrite Physical Analyzer

B: Magnet AXIOM

C: Oxygen Forensic Suite

D: Forensic Toolkit (FTK)

Correct Answer: A
Explanation: Cellebrite Physical Analyzer is a leading tool in forensic circles for creating physical images of iOS devices, allowing for deep data recovery including deleted files, system logs, and hidden files, which are vital for thorough investigations.

----

444. Given the task to identify potential malware on a mobile device, what type of forensic analysis should you perform to scrutinize installed applications and their data?

A: Perform a static analysis on the application binaries to identify any code that does not conform to expected behaviors or contains known malware signatures.

B: Use network analysis to observe outgoing and incoming connections, which can indicate malicious activity but does not analyze the application code itself.

C: Conduct a dynamic analysis by running applications in a controlled environment to monitor behavior, which can be less effective if the malware detects the environment.

D: Implement manual code review for each application, which is time-consuming and requires extensive expertise in mobile app development.

Correct Answer: A

Explanation: Static analysis of application binaries is a direct method to scrutinize the actual code of installed apps for known malware signatures or anomalous behavior patterns, making it highly effective for identifying hidden or obfuscated malicious content without executing the app.

----

445. During a forensic analysis, how would you extract data from a damaged smartphone that can still be recognized by a computer?

A: Utilize JTAG extraction techniques to access memory directly, which is effective even when devices are damaged but still electrically functional.

B: Use cold boot attacks to attempt memory extraction, which is unreliable for damaged devices as it requires the device to operate normally for a brief period.

C: Apply chip-off extraction, which involves physically removing and reading the memory chip, requiring specialized equipment and potentially damaging the chip.

D: Rely on software recovery tools to attempt data extraction through the operating system interface, which may not access all data on a physically damaged device.

Correct Answer: A

Explanation: JTAG extraction is a method used when the device is non-operational but the memory is still intact. This technique allows forensic analysts to access data directly from the device's memory chips, bypassing any damage to the user interface or other hardware components that might prevent traditional data retrieval methods.

----

446. What command in Linux can be used to verify the authenticity of an email by checking its DKIM signature?

A: Use the opendkim-testmsg command to validate the DKIM signature, ensuring the email has not been tampered with during transit.

B: dkim-filter is useful for signing emails with DKIM but does not verify signatures of incoming emails.

C: The mail command can be used to read emails from the terminal but does not perform verification of DKIM signatures.

D: mutt is an email client that supports DKIM verification indirectly through plugins but is not specifically used for command-line DKIM tests.

Correct Answer: A

Explanation: The opendkim-testmsg command is designed specifically for verifying DKIM signatures, a key component in confirming the authenticity of an email, ensuring it hasn't been altered since it was originally sent, which is crucial for forensic purposes.

----

447. In forensic examination, which email header field is essential for tracing the originating IP address of an email sender?

A: The From header shows the sender's email address but does not provide reliable data on the originating IP, which is more relevant in forensic analysis.

B: The X-Originating-IP header may provide an IP address, but it is not consistently included in all emails and can be spoofed or omitted.

C: The Received header is crucial as it contains information about each server the email passed through, including the originating IP.

D: The Return-Path header can sometimes reflect the sender's email address but does not necessarily reveal the originating IP address.

Correct Answer: C

Explanation: The Received header is the most reliable source for tracing an email's journey across the internet, including the originating IP address, which is vital for identifying the source of potentially malicious or phishing emails.

----

448. Fill in the blank: To examine the full path an email took through various mail servers, you should analyze the _____ header field.

A: Received

B: X-Sender

C: Delivered-To

D: X-Received

Correct Answer: A

Explanation: The Received header tracks the complete route taken by an email from sender to recipient, providing a detailed path analysis that is critical for forensic investigations into email origins and the sequence of servers involved.

----

449. How would you verify whether an attachment in an email contains a hidden executable file disguised as a PDF?

A: Utilize the file command on the attachment to check the MIME type, which reveals the true nature of the file, detecting any disguise.

B: Examine the file extension and icon of the attachment for inconsistencies, a method that relies heavily on visual cues and can be easily spoofed.

C: Open the attachment in a secure, isolated virtual machine to observe its behavior, which is more complex and resource-intensive than necessary for just identifying the file type.

D: Run a standard virus scan on the attachment, although this may not detect non-malicious files disguised as another file type.

Correct Answer: A

Explanation: The file command in Linux reads the file header to determine the actual file type regardless of the extension, making it invaluable for identifying files that are not what they appear to be, such as executables disguised as PDFs.

----

450. When analyzing an email for signs of spear-phishing, what method would you use to verify the legitimacy of embedded links without clicking on them?

A: Use a link scanner tool to check the safety of the URL, but this could trigger alerts or download malicious content if not used cautiously.

B: Manually research the root domain of the URL online to assess its reputation, a process that requires considerable time and may not provide immediate risk assessments.

C: Copy and paste the link into a sandboxed browser environment to test the destination, which involves potential risks of exposure to malware.

D: Hover over the link to view the actual URL destination displayed in the email client's status bar, which helps identify misleading links that could lead to malicious sites.

Correct Answer: D

Explanation: Hovering over a link shows the URL in the status bar, providing a safe way to inspect the actual destination without the risk of activating malicious scripts or following through to dangerous websites, which is a fundamental precaution in analyzing phishing attempts.

----

451. What tool can be used to disassemble malware to study its code structure and operation?

A: IDA Pro offers extensive capabilities for disassembling binary files, providing a deep dive into the programming logic and flow of malware.

B: OllyDbg is geared more towards dynamic analysis with debugging features but doesn't provide as extensive disassembly views for static analysis.

C: Ghidra provides some decompilation utilities but lacks the depth required for analyzing more complex malware constructs found in advanced threats.

D: Radare2 is useful for assembly level manipulation and scriptable interface but is less user-friendly and comprehensive than IDA Pro for beginners.

Correct Answer: A
Explanation: IDA Pro is renowned for its comprehensive analysis capabilities, making it a preferred tool for security researchers to dissect complex malware by providing a detailed view of assembly code and program execution paths, which is essential for understanding sophisticated malware operations.

----

452. In a suspected malware file, what command allows you to check the file's hash for quick identification against known malware databases?

A: The file command reveals file type information, but it does not provide the cryptographic hash necessary for malware identification.

B: Running the ls -l command provides basic file details like size and modification date but does not generate any sort of hash value.

C: The md5sum command is another option but is less secure due to vulnerabilities in the MD5 algorithm making it susceptible to hash collisions.

D: Use the sha256sum command to generate a cryptographic hash, which is essential for identifying files in various security databases.

Correct Answer: D
Explanation: The sha256sum command generates a SHA-256 hash of the file, which is a widely accepted standard for malware identification due to its resistance to collisions and security strength, facilitating reliable matching with entries in malware databases.

----

453. Fill in the blank: To monitor malware activity in real time, including system calls and network traffic, _____ can be used effectively.

A: Sysinternals Suite

B: Tcpdump

C: Nessus

D: Wireshark

Correct Answer: D

Explanation: Wireshark is a powerful tool for capturing and analyzing network traffic, making it ideal for observing how malware communicates over the network, tracks data exfiltration attempts, and interacts with command and control servers in real time.

----

454. During a reverse engineering session, how would you extract strings from a binary to find potential C&C server URLs?

A: The cat command outputs the entire file contents to the terminal, which is inefficient for identifying specific strings within large binary files.

B: The grep command can filter out lines in text files but is not as effective at pulling readable text out of binary files without proper patterns.

C: Apply the hexdump tool to view the binary in hexadecimal form, which is useful for examining file structure but less so for extracting clear text data.

D: Utilize the strings command on the binary file to extract readable character sequences that can reveal network addresses, domains, or suspicious keywords.

Correct Answer: D

Explanation: The strings command is specifically designed to pull out printable strings from binary files, which is crucial for uncovering hidden commands, URLs, or other textual indicators that can provide clues about the malware's functionality and external communication points.

----

455. What method should be employed to analyze the behavior of a piece of malware in a safe environment?

A: Using a sandbox environment to test malware allows for automated analysis but might miss deeper system interactions that manual observation can catch.

B: Conducting a live system monitoring with real traffic to simulate actual operating conditions, which can be risky as it might not contain the malware's actions within a secure boundary.

C: Deploy network sniffers to capture traffic generated by malware but this does not allow interaction with the malware's file system or registry changes.

D: Set up a virtual machine with controlled network access to safely observe and analyze malware interactions with the operating system and external servers.

Correct Answer: D
Explanation: Using a virtual machine isolates the malware in a controlled environment, allowing detailed observation of its behavior without risking the integrity of the host system. This method ensures that any harmful actions are contained and provides a safe space for intentional infection to study malware effects and defense mechanisms.

----

456. What command is used to search for specific error codes in a Windows event log file?

A: Use the wevtutil qe Application /q:"*[System[(Level=2)]]" command to query error events in the Application log.

B: The findstr command can locate strings within files but lacks the specific filters needed for effective event log analysis.

C: eventvwr can open the event viewer interface, but it is not suitable for command-line searches or automation of tasks.

D: sc query lists services status but does not interact with event logs for error checking or other log analysis tasks.

Correct Answer: A
Explanation: The wevtutil command is specifically designed for Windows systems to manipulate and query event logs, making it ideal for efficiently finding error codes by applying direct query filters related to event levels or types, crucial for pinpointing issues within the system logs.

----

457. In Unix systems, which command allows you to display the last ten lines of a log file?

A: cat /var/log/syslog | tail -10 effectively shows the last ten entries but is less efficient than directly using tail.

B: The tail -n 10 /var/log/syslog command will display the last ten lines of the syslog file, showing recent entries.

C: The less /var/log/syslog command allows for manual searching but does not directly display the last lines without additional navigation.

D: Using head -n 10 /var/log/syslog shows the first ten lines, which does not help with viewing the most recent log activities.

Explanation: The tail command is fundamental in Unix-like systems for viewing the end of files, making it essential for checking the latest entries in log files, which is typically where the most recent and relevant activities like errors or alerts are logged.

----

458. Fill in the blank: To monitor logs in real time and alert for specific patterns, _____ is often used in Linux environments.

A: awk

B: grep

C: cron

D: sed

Correct Answer: B
Explanation: Grep is a powerful tool used widely in Unix systems for searching text using regular expressions. It allows for real-time log monitoring by combining it with other commands like tail -f, enabling administrators to dynamically watch for specific patterns or potential issues as they are logged.

----

459. How would you identify unauthorized access attempts from a log file containing IP addresses and timestamps?

A: Implement machine learning algorithms to predict unauthorized access patterns, which can be complex and require extensive data training.

B: Review each log entry manually for unauthorized access, which is time-consuming and impractical for large volumes of data.

C: Sort the log file by timestamp and use regular expressions to filter out entries with failed login attempts from unusual IP ranges.

D: Apply a basic text search for "unauthorized access" within the log, which may miss entries that do not use this exact phrasing.

Correct Answer: C
Explanation: Sorting the log entries by timestamp and applying regular expressions to identify failed login attempts from non-standard IP addresses is an efficient method to detect unauthorized access, as it focuses on the exact patterns and anomalies that signify such attempts.

----

460. Which tool would you use to parse large volumes of log data to visualize patterns and anomalies?

A: Employ Elasticsearch along with Kibana to efficiently analyze and visualize trends from large sets of log data.

B: Rely on traditional database queries to extract and analyze log data, which can be cumbersome and lacks real-time processing capabilities.

C: Utilize a simple log viewer tool that allows for manual scrolling through data but does not provide automated analysis or visualization capabilities.

D: Use a spreadsheet program to manually enter and analyze log data, which is labor-intensive and not scalable for large datasets.

Correct Answer: A

Explanation: Elasticsearch, in combination with Kibana, provides a robust solution for handling large volumes of log data. It allows for complex queries, real-time data indexing, and effective visualization, which are critical for quickly identifying trends, patterns, and potential security threats within log data.

----

461. What configuration should be applied in a SIEM to ensure it collects all login and logout events from multiple network devices?

A: Set up SNMP traps for each device to report only critical events, which may not reliably cover all user activity logging requirements.

B: Rely solely on default device configurations, which may not specifically target or effectively capture all relevant log events.

C: Use manual log collection methods periodically, which fails to provide real-time logging and can miss critical events.

D: Configure the SIEM to use agents or syslog forwarding for all devices, applying necessary filters to capture only login-related events.

Correct Answer: D

Explanation: Setting up SIEM agents or configuring syslog forwarding ensures that all relevant log data, particularly login and logout events, are captured from across network devices. This is crucial for maintaining visibility into user activities across the network, enabling effective monitoring and incident response.

----

462. Which protocol is typically used to securely transmit log data from network devices to a SIEM system?

A: HTTP is used occasionally for log transmission but is not recommended due to its lack of encryption and security in transferring logs.

B: The Syslog protocol, especially over TLS, is ideal for secure and reliable log data transport to a SIEM system.

C: The FTP protocol can be used for transmitting log files, though it lacks the necessary security features for sensitive data.

D: SNMP is capable of sending log data but is generally used for device management and monitoring rather than secure log transfer.

Correct Answer: B
Explanation: Syslog over TLS provides a secure method to transmit log data, ensuring that all information sent to the SIEM is encrypted and protected from unauthorized access during transit, which is essential for maintaining data integrity and security.

----

463. Fill in the blank: To create alerts for multiple failed login attempts, the _____ rule must be configured in the SIEM.

A: aggregation

B: threshold

C: pattern

D: correlation

Correct Answer: D
Explanation: Configuring a correlation rule in a SIEM allows it to analyze multiple events collectively, such as repeated failed login attempts, and generate alerts based on these patterns. This is vital for identifying potential security threats, such as brute force attacks, effectively.

----

464. How would you set up a SIEM to automatically respond to a detected threat, such as isolating a compromised host?

A: Employ third-party software to manually trigger isolation after an alert, which introduces potential for delays and errors in threat response.

B: Schedule regular manual reviews of SIEM alerts to decide on the need for isolation, which delays response time significantly.

C: Create an automated response rule within the SIEM that triggers network segmentation or firewall rules to isolate the host based on its IP address.

D: Allow the SIEM to only log and report detected threats without any automated response, reducing its effectiveness in incident management.

Correct Answer: C
Explanation: Automating response actions in the SIEM to isolate a compromised host as soon as a threat is detected minimizes the potential damage and spread of an attack. This proactive approach is critical in rapidly containing and mitigating security incidents.

----

465. What is the most effective way to integrate threat intelligence feeds into a SIEM to enhance its detection capabilities?

A: Use a publicly available, free threat intelligence feed that does not automatically sync with the SIEM, limiting real-time applicability.

B: Implement a direct integration with a threat intelligence platform that automatically updates and applies indicators of compromise (IoCs) to ongoing monitoring.

C: Subscribe to email-based threat intelligence reports and manually input data into the SIEM, inefficient and error-prone.

D: Manually download threat intelligence updates weekly and upload them to the SIEM, which can cause delays in response to new threats.

Correct Answer: B
Explanation: Direct integration of a threat intelligence platform with a SIEM ensures that the latest intelligence is continuously and automatically applied to monitoring processes. This enhances the SIEM's ability to detect advanced threats by using up-to-date IoCs, providing a dynamic defense posture.

----

466. You are tasked with identifying covert communications within encrypted traffic on a corporate network. What command line tool should you employ to detect anomalies based on heuristics?

A: Choose aircrack-ng for network security testing focused on Wi-Fi networks, not suitable for encrypted traffic anomaly detection.

B: Use netsniff-ng, a powerful tool for sniffing network traffic and detecting anomalies in data streams.

C: Opt for tcpdump to capture and analyze packets, but it might not provide heuristic-based detection.

D: Employ wireshark for in-depth packet analysis, but it requires extensive filtering to detect anomalies effectively.

Correct Answer: B

Explanation: netsniff-ng is specifically designed for low-level network monitoring and anomaly detection in traffic, making it suitable for sniffing encrypted communications and identifying unusual patterns through its comprehensive heuristics capabilities.

---

467. While investigating an anomaly in network traffic, you notice unusual outbound connections. Which tool will allow real-time analysis and display of network protocols for threat hunting?

A: snort is an IDS that can detect threats but is not tailored for real-time network protocol analysis.

B: nmap is useful for scanning network ports and identifying services but does not analyze protocol data in real-time.

C: Use tcpview to monitor incoming and outgoing network connections, though it lacks real-time protocol analysis.

D: Employ Wireshark, known for its ability to analyze network packets in real-time and provide insights into potential threats.

Correct Answer: D

Explanation: Wireshark stands out for its comprehensive capability to capture and analyze packets in real time, providing detailed insights into network protocols and traffic patterns which are essential for detecting and understanding threats on the fly.

---

468. In a threat hunting scenario, fill in the blank with the correct Sysinternals Suite tool: "To discover hidden or rogue processes on a host system, a cybersecurity technician should use _____."

A: Autoruns is crucial for detecting rogue processes that auto-start on the system.

B: Process Explorer can visually display active processes but might not reveal hidden or rogue processes effectively.

C: PsExec allows running processes remotely but does not help in identifying rogue or hidden processes on a local machine.

D: PsList shows running processes and their details but lacks the depth to uncover hidden processes automatically.

Correct Answer: A

Explanation: Autoruns from Sysinternals Suite is the most comprehensive tool available for examining all programs configured to run during system bootup or login. It provides the visibility needed to identify any unauthorized or hidden processes, making it an indispensable tool for rooting out malware.

----

469. During a threat hunting task, you encounter persistent malware that has likely modified system files. What PowerShell cmdlet can you use to check for file integrity and find potential modifications?

A: Set-ExecutionPolicy allows changing PowerShell execution policies, irrelevant for file integrity checks.

B: Test-Path cmdlet is useful for verifying the presence of files but does not compare file integrity.

C: Invoke-Command is used to execute commands on remote hosts but won't help in identifying file modifications.

D: Use the Get-FileHash cmdlet to generate hash values of files and compare them to known good values for integrity checks.

Correct Answer: D

Explanation: The Get-FileHash cmdlet in PowerShell is a direct method to verify the integrity of system files by comparing their current hash values against baseline good values. This is crucial in detecting modifications by malware, ensuring that any anomalies are quickly identified.

----

470. A cybersecurity team conducts an exercise to trace the origins of an attack within their network. They have logs from multiple network devices. Which approach is the most effective for correlating events and identifying attack patterns?

A: Implement a centralized log management solution that aggregates logs from all devices, enhancing the ability to correlate data and spot irregular patterns.

B: Utilize decentralized log analysis that requires cross-referencing data from various sources, increasing complexity.

C: Opt for automated attack simulation tools to test network resilience but not effective for real-time attack tracing or log correlation.

D: Rely on manual log review from each device, which can be time-consuming and less effective in identifying sophisticated attacks.

Correct Answer: A

Explanation: Centralized log management systems allow for the aggregation of logs from multiple network devices, enabling efficient correlation and analysis. This approach significantly improves the ability to detect and analyze attack patterns across a distributed network environment, which is crucial for effective threat hunting.

----

471. After a data breach, which command should be used first to isolate a compromised system from the network?

A: Use netstat -r to review routing tables and identify unauthorized entries.

B: Change firewall settings to block all incoming and outgoing traffic temporarily.

C: Execute ipconfig /release to drop the current IP address and cut off network access.

D: Apply route delete to remove potentially harmful routes set up by attackers.

Correct Answer: C

Explanation: The command ipconfig /release is effectively used to immediately drop the system's current IP address, thus cutting off network access and isolating the compromised system. This step is crucial to prevent further data exfiltration or damage.

----

472. What is the first step in restoring data from backups after a ransomware attack has encrypted critical files?

A: Begin immediate restoration of data from the most recent backup without checking its integrity.

B: Perform a verification of the backup data integrity before restoration begins.

C: Retrieve data from cloud backups, assuming it is not affected by the ransomware.

D: Restore the most critical systems first to minimize downtime, regardless of data verification.

Correct Answer: B

Explanation: Before restoring data, it's essential to verify the integrity of the backup data to ensure that it has not been tampered with or damaged. This verification step safeguards against the restoration of corrupted or compromised files, which can prolong the impact of an incident.

----

473. Fill in the blank: To verify the integrity of restored data, use the command _____ to compare checksums.

A: Use diff to compare original files with those that have been restored.

B: chkdsk is typically used for disk errors but can be misapplied for file integrity checks.

C: sha256sum should be utilized to generate and compare checksums of files.

D: md5sum can be used, though it is less secure and not recommended for critical data validation.

Correct Answer: C
Explanation: Using sha256sum to check the integrity of files by comparing their checksums is a reliable method. This command generates a SHA-256 hash of files, which can be compared to pre-incident checksums to ensure that the restored data is accurate and unmodified.

----

474. A cybersecurity technician is planning the recovery process after an incident. Which of the following is the most effective first action to ensure business continuity?

A: Establish a communication plan to inform all stakeholders about the incident and expected recovery steps.

B: Prioritize hardware replacements for all affected machines as a precaution against embedded malware.

C: Rebuild all affected systems from scratch, ensuring no remnants of the incident remain.

D: Resume business operations with minimal system checks to expedite return to normalcy.

Correct Answer: A
Explanation: Establishing a communication plan as a first step helps manage the situation by keeping stakeholders informed and maintaining trust. This strategic communication prevents misinformation and ensures coordinated recovery efforts, which are vital for effective incident management and business continuity.

----

475. During incident recovery, a team discovers that multiple systems are infected with malware. What should be their first step in handling the situation?

A: Update antivirus software and scan all systems to identify and quarantine malware.

B: Segregate the affected systems from the network to prevent the spread of malware.

C: Implement network monitoring tools immediately to detect any further unusual activity.

D: Conduct an immediate company-wide password reset to prevent further unauthorized access.

Explanation: Implementing an immediate company-wide password reset addresses the risk of compromised credentials, which is often overlooked during recovery. This step is crucial to secure access to systems and data, helping to prevent further unauthorized access or lateral movements within the network.

----

476. What command generates a timeline of file activity for forensic analysis in Linux environments?

A: Execute stat to view file status and modification times, but it does not create a comprehensive timeline.

B: Run ls -lR to list files recursively with details but without constructing a timeline of events.

C: Employ find . -type f -printf to list files, which gives detailed file information but not a timeline.

D: Use fls -m with the TSK (The Sleuth Kit) to create a body file for mactime.

Explanation: fls -m creates a timeline by generating a body file that can be processed with mactime, crucial for reconstructing events in forensic analysis. This command line tool is part of The Sleuth Kit, highly regarded for its robustness in handling file system analysis.

----

477. When compiling a forensic report, which tool should be used to ensure the integrity of evidence with cryptographic hashes?

A: Utilize hashdeep to compute and compare MD5, SHA1, and SHA256 hashes of files.

B: Apply sha1sum for hashing, which, like md5sum, lacks multiple hash types and comprehensive comparison features.

C: chkdsk can report on disk status and errors but is irrelevant for forensic integrity verification.

D: Use md5sum to check file integrity, though it only provides MD5 hashes, which are less secure.

Explanation: hashdeep offers a robust solution for verifying the integrity of digital evidence through the computation of multiple cryptographic hashes. Its ability to handle MD5, SHA1, and SHA256 simultaneously allows for thorough and reliable verification, ensuring that forensic data remains untampered.

----

478. Fill in the blank: "To document the state of a network during an incident, a forensic analyst should use the _____ command to capture live network data."

A: wireshark for network data capturing, but it's primarily for in-depth analysis, not instant documentation.

B: tcpdump should be used to capture and analyze packets, documenting network traffic and incidents.

C: ipconfig displays network settings, which is unhelpful for capturing real-time incident data.

D: netstat provides current connections and listening ports, but does not capture live data for analysis.

Explanation: tcpdump is essential for capturing live network data, allowing forensic analysts to document ongoing network traffic and anomalies during security incidents. This tool is widely used in digital forensics for its effectiveness in real-time data capturing and analysis.

----

479. In the context of forensic reporting, what is the most effective method for securely transferring a digital forensic report to a legal team?

A: Employ secure file transfer protocol (SFTP) to encrypt the transmission of the forensic report.

B: Use cloud storage services with encryption, risking exposure to third-party access.

C: Utilize email with encryption, although it may not comply with all legal standards for secure evidence transfer.

D: Send via physical media like USB drives, which, while secure, poses risks of loss or interception.

Correct Answer: A

Explanation: Using SFTP for the secure transfer of digital forensic reports ensures that data remains encrypted over the network, meeting the stringent security requirements necessary when handling sensitive information in legal contexts.

\-

480. You are required to extract and report all user login attempts and security events from a Windows system. Which tool should you use to accomplish this task?

A: wevtutil allows for querying Windows event logs and extracting specific security logs and information.

B: netsh can show active network connections but does not access detailed security event logs.

C: tasklist displays running applications and services but does not report on security events or logins.

D: regedit to access registry settings, inappropriate for extracting login and security event data.

Correct Answer: A

Explanation: wevtutil is a powerful command-line utility on Windows systems that provides extensive capabilities for querying event logs. It is particularly effective for extracting detailed information on user login attempts and security-related events, essential for comprehensive forensic reporting.

\-

481. What command allows you to verify compliance with security logging requirements mandated by the GDPR?

A: Use auditctl to manage rules and watch system calls that access user data.

B: Use logger to manually write custom log entries, but it does not ensure compliance automatically.

C: Run aureport to generate a report from audit logs, though it does not set rules.

D: Apply semanage to adjust SELinux policies to enforce logging, which is more about policy than auditing.

Correct Answer: A

Explanation: auditctl is part of the Linux Audit system, allowing administrators to monitor and record system calls and file accesses, ensuring that personal data handling complies with GDPR's strict logging requirements. It provides direct control over the audit rules, making it essential for compliance.

----

482. In order to comply with HIPAA requirements for securing protected health information (PHI), which tool should be used to encrypt data at rest?

A: Implement dm-crypt with LUKS for robust encryption of disk partitions containing PHI.

B: VeraCrypt provides strong encryption but lacks the centralized management required for HIPAA environments.

C: OpenSSL can encrypt data transmissions but is not specifically used for data at rest.

D: Use BitLocker for Windows systems, but it does not integrate into broader health platforms easily.

Correct Answer: A

Explanation: dm-crypt with LUKS is a powerful tool for encrypting entire disk partitions, ensuring that data at rest is protected in compliance with HIPAA's security requirements. This tool is critical in environments where sensitive health information must be safeguarded against unauthorized access.

----

483. Fill in the blank: "For adherence to SOX regulations, maintaining _____ logs is mandatory to track access to financial records."

A: access control lists are vital, but they do not provide the necessary log information for SOX.

B: audit trail must be properly configured and maintained.

C: transaction logs are important but not sufficient for SOX compliance on their own.

D: user activity logs are crucial but do not exclusively cover financial data.

Correct Answer: B

Explanation: Maintaining audit trail logs is a specific requirement under the Sarbanes-Oxley Act (SOX) for tracking access to financial records. These logs help ensure that all access is recorded and auditable, which is crucial for transparency and accountability in financial operations.

----

484. During an audit for compliance with PCI-DSS requirements, what is the first command you should run to verify that firewall rules do not allow unauthorized access to cardholder data?

A: Use ufw status to check uncomplicated firewall settings, which might not cover all PCI-DSS needs.

B: Check nmap scans of firewall ports, which is more for testing than verifying existing configurations.

C: Execute iptables -L to list all active firewall rules and ensure compliance with policy.

D: Run firewalld --state to see if the firewall is running but does not detail specific rules.

Correct Answer: C
Explanation: iptables -L is a key command for listing all active firewall rules on Linux systems, essential for verifying that only authorized access to cardholder data is permitted under PCI-DSS regulations. This command provides a clear and concise overview of all rules, helping to ensure that no unauthorized rules are in place.

----

485. If a company needs to demonstrate compliance with the NIST cybersecurity framework, what is the most effective first step in the process?

A: Implement continuous monitoring tools, which are part of a broader strategy but not a first step.

B: Conduct an internal security audit, which might not directly address all NIST framework elements.

C: Update cybersecurity policies and procedures, important but not the initial compliance measure for NIST.

D: Establish a comprehensive risk assessment plan to identify vulnerabilities and compliance gaps.

Correct Answer: D
Explanation: Establishing a comprehensive risk assessment plan is the most effective first step in aligning with the NIST cybersecurity framework. This plan helps identify current vulnerabilities and compliance gaps, providing a foundational overview that guides further cybersecurity measures and compliances.

----

486. What feature in Forensic Toolkit (FTK) allows for the decryption of encrypted files when the password is known?
A: Apply FTK's Data Carver for extracting embedded and deleted data from files.

B: Use the built-in Password Recovery Toolkit (PRTK) to attempt cracking encrypted files.

C: Employ the FTK Decryptor utility, which supports various encryption algorithms.

D: Configure FTK to use external decryption tools by integrating third-party software.

Correct Answer: C
Explanation: The FTK Decryptor utility is specifically designed within Forensic Toolkit to handle the decryption of files using known passwords. It supports a wide range of encryption algorithms, making it versatile for various investigative scenarios where encrypted data needs to be accessed lawfully.

----

487. Which component of FTK is primarily used for analyzing Internet artifacts like browser history?

A: Rely on FTK's Mobile Phone Examiner for insights into synced browser data and cookies.

B: Employ FTK Imager to capture a digital image of the drives, focusing on document files.

C: Access the Registry Viewer to analyze user settings and installed applications.

D: Utilize FTK's Internet Examiner Toolkit for comprehensive analysis of web-related activities.

Correct Answer: D
Explanation: FTK's Internet Examiner Toolkit specializes in the analysis of internet artifacts, including browser history, cookies, and downloads. This toolkit is essential for cases where internet usage patterns are crucial to the investigation, providing a detailed and navigable report of web-related activities.

----

488. Fill in the blank: "FTK can generate a detailed _____ report which includes file signatures and metadata."

A: encryption detection report should be generated to identify encrypted files and their algorithms.

B: file hash should be generated to validate the integrity and authenticity of the data collected.

C: activity timeline should be created to track user actions and file accesses over time.

D: system log should be collated to provide insights into system events and error messages.

Explanation: Generating a file hash report is critical in forensic analysis for verifying the integrity of data. This report helps confirm that files have not been tampered with and maintains a chain of custody by providing exact signatures and metadata, essential for legal proceedings.

----

489. When using FTK to perform a keyword search across a suspect's hard drive, what is the best approach to ensure all variations of a keyword are captured?

A: Configure the search to include fuzzy logic, which allows for variations in spelling and partial matches.

B: Apply regular expressions in the search criteria to find exact matches of specified patterns.

C: Set the search parameters to be case sensitive to ensure precision in keyword detection.

D: Utilize the keyword stemming option, which searches for root variations of the specified words.

Correct Answer: A
Explanation: Configuring keyword searches to include fuzzy logic is a powerful method in FTK to capture all variations of a keyword, including common misspellings and partial matches. This approach broadens the search scope and enhances the thoroughness of the investigation, ensuring more comprehensive search results.

----

490. How does FTK facilitate the identification of previously deleted files during a forensic investigation?

A: Engage the FTK's deep scan option, which examines file slack spaces but not deleted files.

B: Utilize the hash analysis tool to compare file hashes with known databases of deleted files.

C: Use the File Recovery feature that scans for known file headers within unallocated space.

D: Implement a file signature mismatch feature to identify files disguised with wrong extensions.

Correct Answer: C
Explanation: The File Recovery feature in FTK is particularly effective for uncovering deleted files. It scans the unallocated spaces of a drive for known file headers, a method that can recover files even after they have been deleted, providing valuable evidence that may otherwise be overlooked in a forensic investigation.

491. What command should be used to create a bit-by-bit copy of a disk for recovery purposes, ensuring no data is overwritten?

A: Utilize tar to back up files, though it is not suitable for bit-by-bit disk copies.

B: Execute rsync to create a synchronized copy of the data, which doesn't perform bit-by-bit imaging.

C: Run dd if=/dev/sda of=/dev/sdb, which copies data but doesn't ensure bad sectors are handled efficiently.

D: Use dd to create a sector-by-sector image of the disk without altering the original data.

Correct Answer: D
Explanation: The dd command is a widely used utility in data recovery that creates a bit-by-bit image of a disk, ensuring that no data is altered or overwritten during the copying process. It is highly effective for making exact copies of disks for forensic and recovery purposes, preserving the integrity of the original data.

----

492. Which data recovery tool allows scanning of a hard drive's file system to identify and recover deleted files?

A: Run Recuva to scan the hard drive, but its capabilities are limited to Windows systems.

B: Use chkdsk to check for file system errors and recover lost files on a Windows system.

C: Employ PhotoRec to search for and recover deleted files from a variety of file systems.

D: Apply WinHex for manual file recovery, though it requires detailed knowledge of file structures.

Correct Answer: C
Explanation: PhotoRec is a specialized data recovery tool that focuses on recovering deleted files by scanning the underlying data and file signatures. It is capable of identifying and restoring files even when the file system is damaged or corrupted, making it a versatile tool for data recovery operations.

----

493. Fill in the blank: To recover lost partitions on a Linux system, the tool _____ can be used to search and restore partition data.

A: gpart is useful for partition management but may not recover lost partitions as effectively as other tools.

B: fsck can repair file system errors, but it will not recover lost partitions.

C: Use lsblk to list block devices, but it is not designed for recovering lost partitions.

D: TestDisk is a powerful utility that specializes in recovering lost partitions and repairing boot sectors.

Correct Answer: D
Explanation: TestDisk is a powerful open-source utility designed to recover lost partitions and repair corrupted partition tables. It is particularly effective in restoring partition data on Linux systems and can also repair boot sectors, making it indispensable in data recovery scenarios.

----

494. A technician is tasked with recovering files from a damaged hard drive with physical bad sectors. What is the most effective method to create a recovery image without causing further damage to the drive?

A: Use clonezilla, but it may not handle physical bad sectors in the same way as other specialized recovery tools.

B: Execute a basic dd copy, though it may fail when encountering physical bad sectors.

C: Create a disk image using ddrescue, which is designed to recover data from drives with bad sectors.

D: Apply xcopy to duplicate files, which will not handle bad sectors or create an image.

Correct Answer: C
Explanation: The ddrescue tool is specifically designed to create a disk image from damaged drives with bad sectors. Unlike the traditional dd command, ddrescue intelligently skips over bad sectors and retries reading them later, preventing further damage to the drive and maximizing the chances of data recovery.

----

495. During a data recovery operation, the technician discovers that the file system is corrupted, and the standard file recovery tools are not effective. Which strategy should the technician employ to recover the raw data from the disk?

A: Use extundelete to recover deleted files from ext file systems, which is limited when the file system is corrupted.

B: Attempt to use ntfsfix to fix file system errors, though it is unlikely to recover raw data.

C: Rely on chkrootkit for searching for signs of a rootkit, but it won't recover raw data from a corrupted file system.

D: Use a low-level data recovery tool like foremost to scan the disk for raw file signatures and extract the data.

Explanation: In cases where the file system is severely corrupted, tools like foremost allow for raw data recovery by scanning the disk for file signatures. This method bypasses the file system entirely, extracting data based on known patterns, which is essential when standard file recovery methods fail due to file system corruption.

----

496. What command can be used to verify if backup files created for disaster recovery are intact and match their original versions?

A: Use sha256sum to compare the hash values of the original files and the backups, ensuring their integrity.

B: Run diff to compare backup files with original files, though it is not as comprehensive as hash-based verification.

C: Apply tar -cvf to archive and compress the backup files, though it doesn't verify file integrity automatically.

D: Utilize md5sum to calculate file hashes, though MD5 is considered less secure for critical disaster recovery checks.

Explanation: The sha256sum command generates a SHA-256 hash for files, which is a secure way to verify that backup files match the original files. By comparing the hash values of the backups to the original files, a technician can confirm that the backups are intact and have not been corrupted, ensuring the reliability of the data during disaster recovery.

----

497. During a disaster recovery process, which utility is most effective for restoring a Linux system from a full system image backup stored on a network server?

A: Employ rsync to restore a system from a backup stored on a remote server, providing network-based synchronization.

B: Use scp to copy files over a network, though it is not ideal for restoring large system images.

C: Implement gparted to manage disk partitions, which may not be ideal for system-wide image restoration from network storage.

D: Use dd to restore a full system image, but it may not handle large network-based backups effectively.

Correct Answer: A

Explanation: The rsync utility is highly efficient for restoring a system from a backup stored on a remote server. It ensures that the data is synchronized between the backup and the system, allowing for a quick and reliable recovery process. It is especially useful for network-based backups, minimizing downtime during the restoration phase.

----

498. Fill in the blank: "To ensure continuous operation of critical business functions, a cybersecurity technician should establish _____ to automatically redirect traffic in case the primary site fails."

A: Rely on static routing tables to manage traffic, which does not offer automatic redirection.

B: Set up a failover cluster, which ensures automatic redirection of traffic to the backup site in the event of a primary site failure.

C: Configure a DNS load balancer to redirect traffic, though it does not provide the same seamless failover as a clustered solution.

D: Implement active-passive server configuration, which involves manual failover procedures for traffic redirection.

Correct Answer: B

Explanation: A failover cluster is essential for ensuring that critical business functions continue operating without interruption. By automatically redirecting traffic to a backup site when the primary site fails, the cluster ensures continuous availability of services, which is a key component of business continuity planning.

----

499. A company has experienced a significant incident and is transitioning into disaster recovery mode. What is the best method to ensure that mission-critical applications remain functional during the recovery phase?

A: Deploy virtualization technology to move mission-critical applications to a cloud-based infrastructure, allowing uninterrupted service.

B: Rely on physical backups of the applications, but physical recovery methods often lead to longer downtime.

C: Perform an application restore using tape backups, which is slower and may not meet the recovery time objectives.

D: Relocate the applications to an offline storage solution, although it may take time to bring them online during recovery.

Correct Answer: A

Explanation: Deploying virtualization technology allows for mission-critical applications to be migrated seamlessly to a cloud-based infrastructure, which helps ensure that the applications remain functional during the disaster recovery phase. This approach significantly reduces downtime and ensures that critical services are available during recovery.

----

500. After a natural disaster has disrupted business operations, what strategy should a business continuity plan include to minimize downtime and restore services as quickly as possible?

A: Engage a warm site, which provides partially prepared infrastructure, reducing recovery time but still requiring setup.

B: Use manual on-site reconstruction, a time-consuming approach that prolongs downtime after a disaster.

C: Establish a cold site, which provides basic infrastructure but requires significant setup time to restore services.

D: Implement a hot site, which is a fully operational backup facility where services can be restored immediately after the disaster.

Correct Answer: D

Explanation: A hot site is a fully operational backup facility that can immediately take over operations after a disaster. This minimizes downtime and ensures that services are quickly restored, making it a critical component of an effective business continuity plan. The ability to switch to a hot site reduces the impact of a disaster on business operations, allowing for a rapid return to normalcy.